DON'T WORRY, MAKE MONEY

Also by the author

DON'T SWEAT THE SMALL STUFF . . . AND IT'S ALL SMALL STUFF

HANDBOOK FOR THE HEART
(WITH BENJAMIN SHIELD)

HANDBOOK FOR THE SOUL
(WITH BENJAMIN SHIELD)

SHORTCUT THROUGH THERAPY

YOU CAN FEEL GOOD AGAIN

YOU CAN BE HAPPY NO MATTER WHAT

DON'T WORRY, MAKE MONEY

SPIRITUAL AND PRACTICAL WAYS TO CREATE ABUNDANCE AND MORE FUN IN YOUR LIFE

RICHARD CARLSON, PH.D.

NEW YORK

Library of Congress Cataloging-in-Publication Data

Carlson, Richard, 1961 May 16–
Don't worry, make money : spiritual and practical ways to create abundance and more fun in your life / Richard Carlson.
p.   cm.
ISBN 0-7868-6321-8
1. Success in business.   2. Businesspeople—Conduct of life.
3. Success.   4. Happiness.   5. Self-actualization (Psychology)
6. Job satisfaction.   7. Work—Psychological aspects.   I. Title.
HF5386.C272   1998
332.024—dc21   97-14459
                                                                        CIP

FIRST EDITION

5   7   9   10   8   6

BOOK DESIGN BY JENNIFER ANN DADDIO

THIS BOOK IS DEDICATED TO

MY FATHER AND GOOD FRIEND, DON CARLSON,

WITHOUT WHOM NEITHER THIS BOOK, NOR ITS TITLE,

WOULD HAVE BEEN CREATED.

THANK YOU FOR YOUR LOVE, GENEROSITY, AND

CREATIVE IDEAS.

I LOVE YOU.

ACKNOWLEDGMENTS

A special, heartfelt thanks to Don Carlson and Marvin Levin; two very special, highly talented, and generous mentors. Your ideas and concepts were enormously helpful, not only in writing this book but throughout my entire life. I don't know where I'd be without you. Also, a great big thanks to Kenny Trout, Steve Smith, and all the folks at Excel Telecommunications who have taught my wife, Kris, and I both so much about what it takes to become successful. And a warm thank-you to Patti Breitman and Linda Michaels, who both help keep me on track in my career, and Leslie Wells, for her continued inspiration and brilliant ideas. Finally, thank you to my incredible family—Kris, Jazzy, and Kenna—for being so patient and supportive while I was writing this book. I love you all so much.

CONTENTS

Introduction   1

1. Remember that the Journey of a Thousand Miles Begins
   with a Single Step   7
2. Give, Give, Give   9
3. Learn the Magic of Nonattachment   11
4. Experience Relaxed Passion   13
5. Get Mileage Out of Reflection   15
6. Pay Yourself First   17
7. Accept the Fact that You Can Make Excuses, You Can
   Make Money, but You Can't Do Both   19
8. Don't Deal With Problems, Transcend Them   21
9. Learn About Moods and Money   23
10. Consider the Possibility that If It Sounds Too Good to
    Be True, It Might Not Be   25
11. Hire Up   27
12. Don't Worry About the Market—Invest in It   31

13.   Become Less Reactive and More Responsive   33

14.   Work on "Knowing" Instead of "Believing"   35

15.   Remind Yourself that Your Life Begins Now   37

16.   Surround Yourself with Experts   39

17.   Be Aware of What You Don't Know and What You're Not Good At   41

18.   Become Aware of the Passion Factor   43

19.   Experiment With the One-Hour Solution   45

20.   Be Prepared to Walk Away from a Negotiation—You Can Usually Go Back   47

21.   Be Willing to Change   51

22.   Spend the Bulk of Your Time on the "Critical Inch" of Your Business or Project   53

23.   Express Your Gratitude Toward Others   55

24.   Leave a Great Impression (Not Just a Good One)   57

25.   Maintain Wealth Consciousness   59

26.   Wait for Inspiration   61

27.   Use the Power of Reflection   63

28.   Laugh at Your Mistakes (and You Won't Repeat Them)   65

29.   Take Your Lunch   67

30.   Ask for What You Want   69

31.   Short Circuit Your Reaction Spirals   71

32.	Eliminate Your Most Self-defeating Belief	73
33.	Keep in Mind that Circumstances Don't Make a Person, They Reveal Him	75
34.	Form a Winning Partnership	77
35.	Let Go of Fearful Thoughts	79
36.	Think BIG!	81
37.	Make Decisions with the Advantage of *Long-Term* Information Instead of the Disadvantage of *Short-Term* Information	85
38.	Know When to Bet, When to Hold, and When to Fold	87
39.	Change What You Can, Accept the Things You Can't	89
40.	Develop Relationships with People Before You Need Something from Them	91
41.	Be Aware of Your Unique "Stacking Order"	93
42.	Don't Panic!	97
43.	Create from the Inside Out	99
44.	Banish Your Doubt	101
45.	Know the Secret of Silence	103
46.	Sock Away Two Years of Living Expenses	105
47.	Give Up Your Fear of Disapproval	107
48.	Keep a List of Bargain Shopping Places in Your Purse or Wallet	109

49. Don't Rely on Too Much Data   111

50. Find a Mentor   113

51. Delight in the Success of Others   115

52. Ask Yourself, Where Is This Decision Likely to Lead?   117

53. Remember the Golden Rule   119

54. Don't Be Frightened to Ask for Referrals   121

55. Know that the Idea "Opportunity Only Knocks Once"
     Is a Big Myth   123

56. Look for Expenditures that Might Be Made
     Cooperatively Instead of Individually   125

57. Shop Carefully with Your Vacation Dollars   129

58. Decide Carefully Between a Fixed and Variable Interest
     Rate on Your Home Mortgage   131

59. Buy Large Deductible Insurance   135

60. Whistle While You Work   137

61. Encourage Creativity in Others and Have Faith in
     Them   139

62. Don't Give Away Your Power   141

63. Charge What You Are Worth   143

64. Listen, Really Listen   145

65. Cultivate Humor and Learn to Smile   147

66. Start a Buyers Club   149

67. Build Up a Large "Trust Fund"   151

68. Sell the Sizzle, Not the Steak   153

69. Go Ahead and Do It   157

70. Be Willing to Take Advice   159

71. Ask Yourself, What Have I Contributed to This Problem?   161

72. Consider that Wisdom May Be Even More Important than IQ   163

73. Eliminate the Words "I'm Not a Salesperson" from Your Vocabulary   165

74. Consider that Busyness Gets in Your Way   167

75. Think About Purple Snowflakes   169

76. Stay Out of Reverse   171

77. Let Go of the Fear that If You're Relaxed or Happy, You're Going to Fail   173

78. Be Aware of Positive Burnout   175

79. Dive In   177

80. Just Once, Try Something Different   179

81. Help Someone Else Succeed   181

82. Persevere   183

83. Consider the Wisdom of Optimism   185

84. Hold on Tightly, Let Go Lightly   187

85.	Be Willing to Apologize	189
86.	Lighten Up	191
87.	Remember that Everything Is Used the Day After You Buy It	193
88.	Keep in Mind that Cheaper Is Not Always Better	195
89.	Don't Be Afraid to Take Baby Steps	197
90.	Remind Yourself that Your Life Isn't Your Enemy, but Your Thinking Can Be	199
91.	Just Do It	201
92.	Resist the Temptation to Continually Raise Your Standard of Living	203
93.	Start a Car Pool	205
94.	Have a Plan	207
95.	Don't Get Lost in Your Plan	209
96.	Stop Commiserating	211
97.	Work at It	213
98.	Create Your Own Luck	215
99.	Don't Forget to Have Fun	217
100.	Don't Sweat the Small Stuff!	219
	Suggested Reading	221

DON'T WORRY,
MAKE MONEY

INTRODUCTION

When Bobby McFerrin first sang his classic song, "Don't Worry, Be Happy," I felt as if he were singing my thoughts to the world. I've spent most of my professional career studying, learning, teaching, lecturing, and writing about happiness and related topics. I've always known that, despite resistance and objections from the more serious segment of society, people have an innate capacity for happiness. And when we are happy, we not only enjoy our lives more than when we are not, but we are far more competent, productive, and creative. Without the internal distractions of anger, depression, frustration, and especially worry, our relationships flourish, stress is diminished, new doors are opened, and our lives run smoothly.

About five years ago I began to realize that the same essential idea applies to success and money. I had been a reasonably successful businessman in several of my own ventures, yet there seemed to be a small but important missing link that was keeping me from realizing my professional and financial goals. There was a part of me that had always been a little unnecessarily cautious, a part of me that worried too much.

I began to look carefully at the people I respected and admired, people who had "made it" in their given fields. I looked at writers, athletes, businessmen and -women, entertainers, speakers, therapists, entrepreneurs, corporate executives, and other professionals. And what I learned amazed me! While there were certainly all types of people—women, men, conservative, liberal, left-brained, right-brained, street smart, Harvard educated, and so on—who had made it really big, there was a thread of consistency that ran through virtually everyone: They didn't worry about money! Interestingly enough, the lack of worry preceded the success, and was not a by-product

1

of it. An inner, unshakable confidence permeated their entire existence. They were creative problem solvers, great negotiators, and clever creators. They had an ability to see the big picture, they knew the formulas for success. And the best part of it all was that, in almost all cases, it appeared that the nonworriers, the successful people I was studying, truly loved their lives and the way they spent their time. They had fun!

I began to apply some of the teachings I had been working with in the field of happiness and self-esteem to my own business life. My life changed, almost instantly. Whereas before I had been quite frightened to speak publicly, I began to love it. The less I worried about the outcome, the better I became at speaking. This translated into more speaking engagements, more book sales, and far more clients for my business. It was as if all of a sudden my time was in greater demand.

I found that the same relationship between less fear and more success existed in my personal investments. As I worried less, I began to expand my knowledge about different kinds of investments and options. Never once did I (or will I) jump into an investment blindly, as some might assume a person would do if he didn't worry; instead, I simply opened my mind to new possibilities. Instead of approaching my financial life with fear, I was beginning to approach it with wisdom. I took more appropriate risks and asked better questions. While my profits grew, I was also learning how to cut my losses—again without too much worry.

So much in my life began to change, especially the way I related to people. Failure didn't concern me as much, criticism was handled in stride, rejection seemed like information to guide me in a new direction instead of something to immobilize me, hurdles seemed less like obstacles and more like opportunities, and everything, all of it, seemed like more fun. I had more energy, worked a lot smarter, surrounded myself with great people and terrific teachers, and watched my creativity and confidence soar. I tried things I never would have dreamed of attempting. Not everything turned to gold, but some of it did. And that which didn't, always turned out to be a great learning experience.

More than all of this, however, the area of life that changed the most was my ability to make money. And miraculously, I was also learning how to help others better. I had always wanted to be of service, and to a certain extent I had been. Yet up to that point I had felt that I could and wanted to do more. But again, fear was getting in the way. As I applied the strategies of worry reduction to my business life, an interesting thing began to happen. I no longer allowed fear to dictate how much I felt I could give. I gave away more, and it always came back to me. So I'd give more. And more would come back. Whether I was giving money, time, ideas, energy, or simply my love, it always came back to help me, too.

In *The Seven Spiritual Laws of Success*, Deepak Chopra discusses this "law of giving." He describes giving and receiving as two sides of the same coin. The more you give, the more you get back. He's right! But you don't give because you want something. You give because giving is its own reward. It's fun. As you learn to worry less, you'll also learn to trust your heart as much or more than your head. While *you* will be doing better in different aspects of your life, you'll also be doing *more* for other people. You'll be far less preoccupied with success; yet ironically, you'll become more successful, much more. You'll trust that everything will be okay. And it will.

Mother Teresa reminds us, "We cannot do great things on this earth. We can only do small things with great love." I have certainly found this to be true. However, I have also discovered, as have thousands of others, that as we worry less we are more *willing* to do those small things with great love. Rather than postponing the giving of our time, energy, ideas, or money, we learn to give freely, from the heart. I've had clients who, for

3

years, wanted to do important volunteer work but were too frightened to do so. They usually felt that they "couldn't afford" the time off from work. They were too frightened that they might lose their job or fall behind. Fear always created some "good" reason that prevented them from reaching out. Yet, invariably, when they banished their fear and took the step, everything worked out for the best. The actions of their heart led to greater personal fulfillment, the helping of others, new friends, even new personal contacts or ideas that turned their own financial lives around. When the circle of fear is broken, we are *all* the beneficiaries.

If you've read any of my other books, you know that I believe strongly in the potential of people. I believe that we are resilient creatures; that we have the capacity for great joy, compassion, and wisdom; that we don't have to "sweat the small stuff." I'm delighted to add to this list my absolute certainty of the correlation between less worry and more success. As you reduce and eventually remove the worry and fear from your life, you will begin to see new options, ways of doing things, and ways of relating to life that were invisible before. You'll have more fun and be able to help more people. You will live the life of your dreams.

If you've read Marsha Sinetar's *Do What You Love, the Money Will Follow*, Stephen Covey's *The Seven Habits of Highly Effective People*, Wayne Dyer's *Real Magic*, Jack Canfield and Mark Victor Hansen's *The Aladdin Factor*, or practically any of the other recent wonderful books on success, you'll find in them elements of the "less worry is better" ideal. In *this* book I will focus specifically on this topic, because I believe it is one of the most important factors of success. And I think that after reading this book, you'll agree. Until you eliminate worry and fear, it is very difficult to implement any strategy for success.

I will share with you specific strategies to banish worry from your life forever. Whether you want the confidence to pursue a new career or dream;

the emotional freedom to ask others for help; the ability to handle criticism or rejection with ease; the confidence to take a risk, speak to a group, ask for a raise; do more for your favorite charity; invest in a business; or creatively market a service or product, this book will help you.

I cannot adequately put into words how wonderful life can be when worry is diminished. For me, abandoning worry has opened a world of possibilities for both my inner and outer worlds. Life without worry has opened new doors and created freedom that, until a few years ago, I never thought were possible. So, "don't worry"—I know this can happen for you, too.

1.

REMEMBER THAT THE JOURNEY OF A THOUSAND MILES BEGINS WITH A SINGLE STEP

I can vividly remember the first sentence I ever wrote in my very first book! It seems like a long time ago. Yet had I not written that first sentence, I wouldn't have finished that first book, or the second, and so on. And so it goes. Every journey, however long it may be, begins with a single step. But you *must* take that first step. Once you do, each step takes you closer and closer to your goal.

Sometimes, when you consider taking on a new venture—whether it's raising a child, writing a book, starting a new business, beginning a savings plan, or anything else—the task can seem overwhelming. It's as though you'll never be able to arrive at your final destination, as if the first step isn't going to help. When you look too far out toward the horizon, it can seem too difficult. You might even wonder where to begin.

The trick to success sounds very simplistic, because it *is* very simple: Just begin. Take a single step, followed by another, and then another. Don't look too far out into the future, and don't look too far back either. Stay centered in the present moment as best you can. If you follow this simple plan, you'll be amazed at what you can accomplish over time.

When I graduated from my Ph.D. program, my dear friend Marvin gave me, as a gift, the complete works of Carl Jung. That's twenty-six long volumes of material. In volume one was a note from Marvin worth sharing here. He wrote: "Becoming educated doesn't happen overnight! Education is a lifelong process that happens in short intervals. If you were to read only eight pages a day, for the next seven years, you would be one of the world's most knowledgeable experts on the work of Carl Jung, *and* you would get through every page!" Despite not being a huge fan of Jung, I have always appreciated my friend's message.

The same, of course, is true with all ventures. A wealthy friend of mine, worth many millions of dollars, remembers opening his first savings account with his wife over forty years ago with $10. They both laugh when they say, "It's amazing what a little time will do." Had they not decided to start somewhere, their incredible success would never have manifested itself.

Over and over again I hear people telling me about the book they are *going* to write, the savings account they are *about* to open, the business they are *going* to start, or the charity they are *planning* to help. But, in many instances, these plans and dreams keep getting put off until "the conditions are right." One of the most powerful messages I can share with you, one that I'm absolutely certain of, is this: In almost all cases, the conditions you are waiting for will *not* be significantly different next week or next year. Don't worry that the conditions have to be perfect. The truth is, you are *still* going to have to take that first step! If you take it now, instead of later, you'll be many steps closer to your dreams by this time next year. Congratulations, you've just taken the first step in the completion of this book!

2.

GIVE, GIVE, GIVE

Many of us have heard the expression "Giving is its own reward." And while this is certainly true, and more than reason enough to give, there's another aspect of giving that many fail to recognize. Giving is an energy that not only helps others but creates even more for the person who is doing the giving. This is a natural law that is true regardless of whether the person who is giving wants or even realizes what is occurring.

Money is "circulation." It needs to flow. When you are frightened, selfish, or when you hoard everything for yourself, you literally stop the circulation. You create "clogged pipes," making it difficult to keep money flowing back in your direction. Any success you have is despite your lack of giving, not because of it. The way to get the flow going again is to start giving. Be generous. Pay others well, tip your waitress that extra dollar. Support several charities. Give back. Watch what happens! Things will start popping up out of nowhere.

The same dynamic is true if you want to fill your life with love or anything else worthwhile. Giving and receiving are two sides of the same coin. If you want more love, or fun, or respect, or success, or anything else, the way to get it is simple: give it away. Don't worry about a thing. The universe knows what it's doing. Everything you give away will return, with interest!

3.

LEARN THE MAGIC OF NONATTACHMENT

Without realizing it, many of us confuse nonattachment with not caring. In actuality, the two are completely different. Not caring suggests apathy: "I couldn't care less. It doesn't matter to me." Nonattachment, on the other hand, means: "I'll do everything possible, I'll put the odds in my favor, I'll work hard and concentrate. I'll do my best to succeed. *But*, if I don't, that's okay, too."

Being attached to an outcome, holding on, takes an enormous amount of energy, not only during an effort but often after an effort is complete, after you've failed, or been let down, or were dealt a bad hand.

Being nonattached, however, creates emotional freedom. It means holding on tightly but letting go lightly. It suggests trying hard, really caring, but at the same time being completely willing to let go of the outcome.

Attachment creates fear that gets in your way: What if I lose? What if the deal doesn't go through? What if I'm rejected? What if, what if, what if . . . Your belief that everything must work out exactly as you want it to with no glitches creates enormous pressure. Everything rides on your success.

Nonattachment, on the other hand, works like magic. It allows you to have fun in your efforts, to enjoy the process. It helps you succeed at whatever you are doing by giving you the confidence you need. It takes the pressure off. You win regardless of the outcome. The act of *not* worrying helps you focus and stay on purpose. It helps you stay out of your own way. You know in your heart that, even if things don't work out the way you hope they will, everything will be all right. You'll be okay. You'll learn from the experience. You'll do better next time. This attitude of acceptance helps you move on to the next step in your path. Rather than being lost or immobilized in disappointment or regret, you simply move on—with confidence and joy.

4.

EXPERIENCE RELAXED PASSION

Most people would agree that having passion for one's work is a helpful, if not necessary, ingredient for success. Many of these same people, however, confuse useful passion with hyper or frenetic behavior.

Passion takes different forms. It can be the feeling of being driven to success, of rolling up your sleeves, or working long, hard hours. This "hyper" passion can be very exciting, even addicting. The problem with it, though, is that it drains your energy and can be very exhausting. It's generated from external sources, from tight deadlines and big deals. Because of the external nature of this type of passion, a tint of fear always goes along with it: "I love this as long as everything works out well." This type of passion also lends itself to boredom. The only time you're having fun is when there's something on the line, when something exciting is happening. The rest of the time can seem like a letdown. You spend your time waiting and looking for more excitement.

Another, calmer type of passion is what I like to call relaxed passion. This is a contained, "time-release" type of feeling that permeates everything you do. It brings joy and great success to virtually anything. Rather than being frenetic, this feeling is more like exhilaration and enthusiasm. It's a much calmer version of excitement. It can be described as excitement without the worry: "I love this simply because I'm absorbed in what I'm doing."

The way to bring forth this type of passion is to learn to keep your attention fully in the present moment. Try to do only one thing at any given moment and give that "one thing" your full and complete attention. If you're on the phone, stay focused, be "with" the person to whom you are speaking. Don't let your mind drift; be there. If your mind does wander, gently bring it back to the present moment.

Almost anything we do—preparing a report, speaking to a group, solving a problem, generating an idea, doing a difficult task, and so forth—is a potential source of relaxed passion. And it comes not from exciting, external ventures but from our own attention, our own thinking. Too many of us live in moments past or moments yet to be. When our mind is not right here, in this moment, we suck the joy out of an experience. You can bring passion back into your life and your business dealings by simply being more oriented in the present moment. Your focus and insight will be greatly enhanced, as will your ideas and creativity.

5.

GET MILEAGE OUT OF REFLECTION

The ability to honestly and quietly reflect on one's life is one of the most powerful tools for personal growth. Reflection means to bring to life the truth of what's really going on. It's similar to meditation in that you are allowing the truth of the moment, without bias or personal agenda, to surface.

Reflection allows you to see your own contribution to a problem, the ways you might improve, and the blind spots in your thinking. It helps you eliminate any tendency you might have to blame others for your mistakes, make excuses that don't serve you, and break free of old habits.

My wife, Kris, an accomplished businesswoman, incorporates the power of reflection into her daily life. She sits quietly and allows her own wisdom to offer her advice and suggestions on ways she might improve herself and/or her performance. In this way, rather than repeating mistakes, as so many of us do, she makes graceful adjustments that guide her toward success.

To incorporate reflection into your business life, all you need is the desire to do so. You must have a sincere willingness to be honest with yourself and the ability to turn off your internal chatter for a few minutes each day. As you begin to sit quietly, you will notice insights rising to the surface of your mind. Take quiet note of each insight, and store each in your memory. Very soon you'll be on your way to new heights and adventures.

6.

PAY YOURSELF FIRST

On the surface, this is one of the least original ideas in this book. The idea of paying yourself first—before anyone else—is a concept that is often talked about. Most financial professionals realize that it's virtually impossible to accumulate great wealth without this type of discipline and wisdom. The idea is that, if you wait until everyone else is paid before you pay yourself, you'll never get around to it. There won't be anything left. Despite its importance, however, a very small percentage of people actually implement this strategy. The major reason: worry.

If you are worried about having enough, you never will! Fear will prevent you from taking the obvious steps that are needed to create abundance. Thus, one of the first and most important steps you need to take is to nip your worry in the bud.

From this moment on, make a commitment to yourself that you will ignore all thoughts of worry and pay yourself first—before *anyone* else. Every day, or week, or month—whatever is appropriate for you—write yourself a check. Invest in yourself. Trust in yourself. You will have enough for everything else.

You'll be surprised, but somehow, regardless of your income, there will always be enough left to pay your bills. You'll make invisible, wise adjustments in your spending habits. You'll make new choices. And in a very short amount of time, you'll get into the habit of always paying yourself first, saving or investing something for you. You'll watch your savings and net worth grow. As this happens, you'll see how destructive worry can be and how unnecessary it was all along. This will create even more confidence, which will translate into more discipline, creativity, and new ideas. You will find yourself in a new mind-set, creating wealth.

It's critical to realize that you won't stop worrying simply because your income rises. There are plenty of people with enormous incomes who worry all the time. The trick is to trust, without any doubt whatsoever, that the magic works in the other direction. You need to stop worrying, first, and *then* you'll do what it takes to create the abundance you deserve.

7.

ACCEPT THE FACT THAT YOU CAN MAKE EXCUSES, YOU CAN MAKE MONEY, BUT YOU CAN'T DO BOTH

My wife, Kris, is a super businesswoman and a terrific motivator in her home-based business. She works with a company where about 5 percent of the people make about 95 percent of the money. She is one of the 5 percent.

One of the most popular phrases throughout the business has also turned out to be one of the most helpful in moving people toward that 5 percent. That phrase is: You can make excuses, you can make money, but you can't do both. To be honest, when I first heard it, I felt it was a little harsh. Upon closer examination, however, I realized that it wasn't harsh at all. In fact, it's an excellent prescription for less worry, and a helpful tool for success and abundance.

If you think about it, "excuses" are often nothing more than an expression of fear: "I'm frightened that I don't have time," or "I'm afraid to step out of my comfort zone," or "I'm afraid of what people will think," or "I'm afraid I can't do it," or "I don't think it's in my nature." When you remove the fear behind these excuses (when you stop worrying), you create the space and confidence to move forward.

Successful people with full lives must face the same frustrations, hurdles, and fears as everyone else. The difference is in the way they handle their fear. Rather than feeling defeated or immobilized by their fears and worries, successful people conquer them. As Susan Jeffers suggests by the title of her book, they *Feel the Fear and Do It Anyway*! After all, courage is best described as being afraid and "doing it anyway."

19

A person who is in the habit of making excuses keeps himself from his greatest potential. When an excuse enters the mind of this type of person, he attaches himself to the thought, takes it very seriously, thinks about why the excuse is valid, and then uses it as ammunition against himself. It all happens very quickly, usually without the person being aware of it. This is a self-defeating habit that can be broken with a slight shift in one's thinking.

Virtually every successful person I know admits to being confronted, often, with his or her own internal excuses, such as, I'm tired, I'll do it later, or I'm scared, or I don't want to do this. What these people are able to do, however, is to think of their fears and excuses as nothing more than frightening or lazy thoughts that can be overlooked, dismissed, or at least not taken so seriously. Thus, rather than becoming overwhelmed by negative internal dialogue, they are able to stay focused on what they are doing and what they are attempting to accomplish.

8.

DON'T DEAL WITH PROBLEMS, TRANSCEND THEM

When I suggest that clients *not* work on problems, they often appear irritated, as if I'm telling them not to bathe or brush their teeth! This is because most people assume that the only way to solve problems is to work on, or struggle, with them. I have found, however, that focusing on problems is one of the key ways of keeping them alive—as well as preventing you from moving past them. Focusing on problems is also a key ingredient keeping people stuck in worry.

I can assure you that there is a way to get from where you are to where you want to be *without* focusing on problems. It's a natural, virtually effortless, yet far more effective alternative to the usual "roll up your sleeves and solve this problem" manner of dealing with issues.

Recently I knelt down to clean up some glass and a piece got stuck in my knee. I ended up at the urgent care center getting ten stitches. We all know that the worst thing I could possibly do to the healing process would be to poke or pick at my scab. A wiser method is to treat the wound gently, creating the best possible healing environment. Miraculously, the wound will heal all by itself.

Most problems can and should be dealt with in a similar manner. The thoughts we have around our various issues—business and otherwise—create and trigger emotional reactions. What usually happens is that we spend our time and energy dealing with these reactions instead of the actual issue. Simply put, when we are frightened, angry, or impatient, we lose our bearings and get in our own way. Instead of bringing out the best in ourselves and others, we bring out negativity and squeeze out creativity.

Deep down, we all know that for every problem there *is* a solution.

Many times, the solution is obvious to a dispassionate observer, which is the primary reason corporations as well as entrepreneurs hire outside consultants. Often, the reason we cannot see these obvious solutions is that we are trapped in our emotional reactions and habitual ways of seeing life.

The alternative to dealing head on with problems is to clear your mind instead of filling it with painful, confusing details. Quiet down, reflect, and listen. Allow your wisdom, that softer part of your thinking, to surface. More often than not, seemingly out of nowhere, you will have an insight, an answer to your problem. You may be shocked or even struggle with how easy this process is to implement. Nevertheless, the less you worry about your problems, the easier they will be to solve!

9.

LEARN ABOUT MOODS AND MONEY

Moods are one of those unavoidable, mysterious parts of life that must be dealt with by everyone. Our understanding of moods greatly affects not only our wisdom and perspective but our overall level of satisfaction as well. Generally speaking, when our mood is high, our spirits are up. When our mood is low, our spirits are down. Moods are like the weather, constantly changing.

The implications of moods as they relate to money are significant. When we are low, we think of our dissatisfactions more than when we feel good. We worry! We compare ourselves to others and convince ourselves that others are doing better than we are. We focus on our belief that making money is hard work. Perhaps we believe that there isn't enough money or opportunity to go around, or that people are selfish and out for themselves.

The fascinating thing about moods is that, to a large degree, we only believe these negative, fearful, and self-defeating thoughts when our mood is low. When our mood is high, we think very differently. We don't worry as much. Rather than believing that others are doing better than we are, or even spending energy comparing ourselves to them, we realize that we are all on different paths, doing the best we can. Instead of complaining that making money is hard work, we get a kick out of the entire process and see new ways to create abundance for ourselves and others. Rather than seeing limitations in the supply of money, we know that there is plenty to go around. Finally, instead of seeing people as selfish and out for themselves, we realize that most people are very generous and giving. And those who aren't have simply lost touch with their heart.

So what do you do? The trick is to be grateful when your mood is high and graceful when it is low. Try to keep in mind the effect your mood is having on the way you are thinking and feeling. Your understanding of moods allows you to keep your perspective and not take so seriously the thoughts you are having when you are low. Rather than believing in your negative and fearful perceptions, you can dismiss them as being mood-related.

The same dynamic applies to your creativity and your ability to create abundance. When you are in a low mood, don't make important business (or life) decisions. Don't force it. Your thinking and wisdom are not as sound as they will be in a higher state of mind.

Resist the temptation to worry about your moods. Moods are always changing, and yours could change at any moment. Simply realizing that you are stuck in a mood usually raises your spirits. Again, don't worry! As your mood rises, your capacity to create will unfold.

10.

CONSIDER THE POSSIBILITY THAT IF IT SOUNDS TOO GOOD TO BE TRUE, IT MIGHT NOT BE

The old adage "If it sounds too good to be true, it probably is" isn't always correct. In fact, the suspicion, cynicism, and doubt that are inherent in this belief can and does keep people from taking advantage of excellent opportunities.

Cynicism contradicts abundance. Cynics, critics, and doubters are clouded by their own destructive, self-defeating filters that say things like "That can't work," "That's impossible," or "It's too good to be true." These people are big-time worriers. They're concerned with what other people think, and they are stuck in doing things "the right way," the same way everyone else does them. These people have closed minds that are fixated on the status quo.

I was lucky enough to hear about a great stock from a good friend of mine. He told me and four others what he knew about it. Unfortunately for my other friends, they were true cynics. "Sure," they all said in a sarcastic tone, "I'll bet it's a great deal." They instantly dismissed the suggestion. I've learned, however, to keep an open mind. And while I would probably decide to buy less than one stock in every hundred that I hear about, I'm always willing to take a look. It took me less than an hour to do a little research on the stock, and I decided to buy some shares. Lo and behold, the stock doubled in less than a month. Lucky? Of course. But had I not been open-minded, I wouldn't have been in a position to be lucky!

If you think something is too good to be true, you'll be very hesitant to take a careful look at it, and you'll dismiss it as being superficial or too risky. What happens, however, if you're wrong? You'll miss out. Often there are great deals and wonderful opportunities that come your way. But to take advantage of them, you must be open, willing to take a look, learn something new, try something different. Obviously, this doesn't mean you jump into risky ventures or avoid careful consideration, but it does mean that sometimes, you have to do something a little differently to do a little better, to have a little more.

Being a nonworrier doesn't guarantee success, but it sure makes it easier to spot great opportunities when they come your way. You'll be far more open to taking a look, to considering new options, new ways of doing things, marketing products or services, or taking an uncharacteristic risk. By becoming a less cynical, more open-minded nonworrier, you'll bring far more joy into your work and open the door to far more abundance in your business and career.

11.

HIRE UP

If you want to talk about a strategy that is 100 percent related to less worry, this is it. The concept of hiring up is critical to your success. Essentially, hiring up means you hire and work with people that are more qualified than you. That's right, *better* than you.

It won't come as a surprise to very many of you that the factor that prevents people from subscribing to this philosophy is fear. The fear that "I can be replaced" or "someone might be better than me."

Do you ever wonder why so many businesses operate as if no one knows what they're doing? Sometimes the answer is that no one really does know what they're doing. Take a typical small business that is based on fear. Picture the manager who is responsible for hiring the people she works with. If she's frightened of being replaced or overshadowed, she's likely to hire people who aren't quite as bright or competent as she is. In all likelihood, she won't even be aware of her hidden agenda to keep the business down, but that's precisely what she'll do. She was hired not so much for her expertise in running the business but for her efforts in *building* a successful business. But what she's doing is surrounding herself with people even less qualified than herself because she believes she'll look better. Businesses based on fear are doomed to failure.

People who are self-employed often fall into the same trap. "I can do this myself better than anyone else" is really a foolish statement based on fear. It's ridiculous to spend your time doing things that others can do better, because your time is better spent doing the things that you're really good at. The truth is, none of us are experts at everything, but most of us are good at something. A simple example would be that if you can consistently earn $50 an hour doing whatever it is you do, then it makes more sense for you to keep doing it and to hire someone to do the time-consuming job of keeping your books and records. That way you don't waste valuable income-earning time—and you'll probably be better organized than if you'd done it yourself.

A very successful friend once joked that he couldn't afford "the luxury" of driving from San Francisco to the Pacific Northwest, despite the fact that airline fares were high at the time. He would much rather pay the airline to do what they do best—get him where he needs to be quickly—than spend twelve or more hours in the car missing out on untold opportunities for success and building his business.

As you let go of worry and "hire up," some magical things begin to happen. You begin to get out of your own way and allow success to unfold. One of the turning points in my career was when I realized that, although I believe I'm an excellent writer, I'm not always such a great editor. As I let go of the fear that an editor could change my essential message, I began to experiment with working with various editors. I started to "hire up." Guess what? They didn't change my message, they improved it. And to top it off, a good editor could clean up my writing in a fraction of the time that I spent struggling with it, giving me far more time to do what I do best.

As you let go of fear, you will find that you will be rewarded for your willingness to reach out. Rather than losing your job, you'll be praised for contributing to the success of your business. The truth is, if you can become one of the few people who operates not out of fear but out of a sincere willingness to do what's in the best interest of your business, you'll become an indispensable part of that company's success. And if for some strange and unlikely reason your good faith efforts are not appreciated and rewarded, you will know beyond any doubt that you aren't working in the best possible environment. Don't worry. When you're thinking in "hire up" terms, another, better opportunity is just around the corner.

A good definition of an entrepreneur is someone who can achieve predetermined goals through the efforts of himself and others. Why not raise the standards of those results by hiring up? The quality of your work will improve, and your profits will explode.

12.

DON'T WORRY ABOUT THE MARKET—INVEST IN IT

I believe that one of the closest things to a worry-free, wealth-building strategy is to invest, *long term*, in the stock market, preferably through your company 401K or, if you're self-employed, your SEP. Why? Because historically, to profit from this simple, well-known strategy, it doesn't matter in the short term if the market is going up or down. You win either way. There is absolutely nothing to worry about.

Once you commit to the "don't worry" attitude, you'll chuckle as you notice how many people worry, every day, unnecessarily, over which direction the market is moving. "What a relief, the market is having a good day" and "Oh no, the market is down" are frequent comments, but in reality, they have virtually no relevance if you are investing for the long term.

What is there to worry about? By implementing the "pay yourself first" strategy, by investing a predetermined percentage, such as 10 percent of your income to yourself (into high-quality, no-load mutual funds), you virtually guarantee that, over time, you'll amass a small fortune. You simply put the money in, month after month, and leave it there.

If the market is going up, your investment is worth more money. Congratulations, you win. But if the market is going down, your next investment will afford you the luxury of purchasing more shares of stock at a lower price. Congratulations, you win again!

To top off this worry-free, wealth-building strategy, you can get the federal and state governments to pitch in a third, or even more, of your total investment. By using a company retirement plan or self-employed SEP, you can deduct your contribution from your taxable income up to a certain maximum limit, saving you thousands of dollars and reducing the out-of-pocket costs of your investment. Your tax adviser, or even a knowledgeable friend, can probably show you how simple it is to accumulate wealth using this strategy and how to maximize the government's contribution toward your financial goals. The point here, however, is to show you that "don't worry" is not simply a cliché. There are many worry-free, practical approaches to building your fortune; this is simply one of the best. As always, your external success begins with your attitude toward life.

13.

BECOME LESS REACTIVE AND MORE RESPONSIVE

In business and in life, we have essentially two psychological modes that we are in most of the time: reactive and responsive. The reactive mode is the one that feels stressful. In it, we feel pressured and are quick to judge. We lose perspective and take things personally. We're annoyed, bothered, and frustrated.

Needless to say, our judgment and decision-making capacity is severely impaired when we are in a reactive state of mind. We make quick decisions that we often regret. We annoy other people and tend to bring out the worst in them. When an opportunity knocks, we are usually too overwhelmed or frustrated to see it. If we do see it, we're usually overly critical and negative.

The responsive mode, on the other hand, is our most relaxed state of mind. Being responsive suggests that we have our bearings. We see the bigger picture and take things less personally. Rather than being rigid and stubborn, we are flexible and calm. In the responsive mode, we are at our best. We bring out the best in others and solve problems gracefully. When an opportunity comes our way, our mind is open. We are receptive to abundance.

Once you are aware of these two drastically different modes of being, you will begin to notice which one you are in. You'll also notice the predictability of your behavior and feelings when you are in each mode. You'll observe yourself being irrational and negative in your reactive mode and calm and wise in your responsive state of mind.

Simply becoming aware of the different dynamics of your mind will open the door to tremendous changes in your life. You'll begin to notice when you fall into a reactive state of mind. You'll feel your own impatience. When this happens, simply say to yourself, "Whoops, there I go again" or something to this effect. Any type of simple acknowledgment will do the trick. You'll discover, as you notice and acknowledge your own reactivity, coupled with your understanding that, in all cases, it pays to be more responsive, you'll quickly come out of a reactive mode and fall into a more responsive state of mind.

A responsive state of mind is fertile ground for success. When your mind is clear and relaxed, you pave an open channel for abundance and joy. There is a direct and clear relationship between how much time you spend in a responsive state of mind and your own level of success. The more you are able to stay out of reactivity, the more opportunities will present themselves. Beginning right now, use the power of responsiveness to create your own success.

14.

WORK ON "KNOWING" INSTEAD OF "BELIEVING"

When you believe something, it's usually due to the fact that someone told you so—your parents, an instructor, a friend, a colleague, a partner, boss, or employee. You were influenced, often in a positive way, by what you were told. Consequently, your belief system was formed, altered, or solidified in some measurable way. For example, your parents may have attempted to convince you that holding a corporate job was more important, held more status, and had a more secure future than being a gardener. If you believed them, you would have factored this concept into your career decisions and the directions you followed. Every one of us has beliefs and there is certainly nothing wrong with this.

Knowing, on the other hand, is intrinsic in nature. When you know something, you feel it. You are certain. You may not always be able to explain or articulate why you feel the way you do, but something within you—wisdom, common sense, guidance, whatever—is providing you with needed answers and guiding you in a direction, as long as you listen.

For example, I always knew that I would be a teacher of some kind. I knew that my calling or role as an adult was to be sharing what I knew to be true through writing and speaking. This is difficult to explain because I believed I was an inadequate writer and was terribly frightened to speak in public. In fact, I nearly flunked high school English and had actually fainted while attempting to speak in front of a group! Perhaps the *only* thing I did right was listen to my inner voice—the source of knowing. It kept insisting that, despite appearances to the contrary, somehow I was going to teach. It took many years, but, as is always the case, knowing is more powerful than believing. Eventually I was guided in the direction I now call my career—writing, speaking, and teaching.

All of us have things that we know to be true about ourselves—dreams that we have, gifts we wish to share, unique talents we want to pursue. But all too often we bury these things we know with our own beliefs, and ultimately they become our limitations. Our beliefs convince us of things like: I can't do it, or It's for someone else, or It's not in my nature. Or they provide us with convenient excuses: I don't have time, or I never get any breaks, or My life isn't set up right.

The good news is that, the moment you decide that what you *know* is more important than what you have been taught to *believe*, you will have shifted gears in your quest for abundance. Success comes from within, not from without. It begins by listening to your inner calling and wisdom. What do you truly value and enjoy? What is your heart trying to tell you? Is there something that you have an inner need to pursue? These are the types of questions that will put you on your path toward greatness. Once on that path, you will discover your own unique way to make the path an enormous success and a great deal of fun. I've seen people turn hobbies into fortunes, change careers completely, start side businesses, or magically transform their existing career by changing their attitude. Over and over again, I have seen people turn dreams into realities through a simple shift in perspective. How this process unfolds is up to you. The path will be clear when you listen to your own inner voice.

15

REMIND YOURSELF THAT YOUR LIFE BEGINS NOW

One of the most severely limiting beliefs that many of us have is that the person we were yesterday is the person we have to be today. This belief keeps us tied to our past mistakes, habits, and limitations. We somehow buy into the notion that history truly does repeat itself, that if we weren't successful yesterday, we certainly can't be successful today or tomorrow.

If you can see how ridiculous and self-defeating this belief is, you can make an instant shift toward success and fulfillment. All of us have unlimited potential and a clean slate in this moment—now. What prevents us from tapping into this potential is our own mental ties to the past. Letting go of your past is like taking a set of heavy chains from around your neck. It frees you to pursue your dreams and rise to your greatest potential.

I heard a wonderful story about the power of living in the present moment. It involves imagining that you are on a boat in the middle of the ocean. You are standing at the helm, heading due east, as you ask yourself three important questions: First, what is the wake? You turn back and observe the water behind the boat that is left behind. The wake is that water. It forms a shape *behind* the boat until it disappears into nothingness. Second, you ask yourself the question, Can the wake drive the boat? You quickly answer, "Of course not. That's preposterous." The wake has no power. Finally, you ask yourself, What then powers the boat? You think for a moment and come to the obvious conclusion. All of the power of the boat comes from the present-moment energy of the engine. That's it. There is nothing else.

The analogy to your own life is clear. Your present-moment energy is all you need. It's incredibly powerful and resourceful. The problem is, many of us don't use our present-moment energy to its fullest because we are constantly trying to use our "wake," that which is behind us, our past, to move us forward. But like the wake in the ocean, our past has no power. It is nothingness.

Our past has no power other than the power we give it. One of the most dynamic and significant changes you can make in your life is to make the commitment to drop all negative references to your past, to begin living now. Operate as if all the power in your life begins and ends in this moment. The positive energy you create may shock you. New doors and opportunities will open. As your past habits creep into your consciousness, simply acknowledge them and let them go. This is not a complicated process, and you can begin doing so immediately. Your past was important because it was needed to get you into the present. Your life, now, is a series of present moments to be experienced, one after another. Focus on what you can do today, right now in this moment, and you will have already begun to create the abundance that is your birthright.

16.

SURROUND YOURSELF WITH EXPERTS

Charles Givens, author of the phenomenally successful book *Wealth Without Risk*, has said, "If you want to learn about money, learn from someone who has a lot of it." So, many people surround themselves with "successful" people, "experts" on making money, and people who have a lot more money than they do. Yet they are intimidated by them, frightened that people who are more successful won't be willing to spend time or share their ideas with us. Nothing could be farther from the truth. The reality is, accomplished people love it when someone takes an interest in their success; they love to share their wisdom, good ideas, or business secrets. It makes them feel wanted and needed.

Two of my favorite people in the world each have a great deal of money. One is entirely self-made, the other comes from inherited wealth. Both are exceptionally willing to sit down and share ideas with me, or practically anyone else who asks them. The interesting thing, however, is that they both claim that very few people have the courage to ask to pick their brains for ideas. What a waste! I probably know, personally, over a hundred super-successful people, and I can't think of a single one whose door isn't almost always open for others. I've worked on projects with some very famous, successful people through some of my other books. When people ask me, "How in the world did you convince them to participate?," they are often shocked at the simplicity of my answer. I respond honestly by saying, "I just asked them." You'll be amazed at the number of people who are more than willing to help, whether it's the owner of a successful grocery store, a top-producing insurance salesperson, a well-known author, a physician, a lawyer, or an excellent teacher. Most want and are willing to offer advice. In fact, asking someone you admire and respect for their feedback and ideas is the greatest compliment you can offer them.

Not all, but most highly successful people (in any field) are available to help others. Usually, it's the people fighting to climb to the top who are the most frightened, insecure, or unwilling to offer guidance. If you do ask for help or advice and are turned down, you can bet that the next person you ask will be more than willing. If you want great advice and you want to avoid big mistakes, seek help. Surround yourself with winners. Don't get advice from Uncle Charley unless he, himself, is a successful person. Go straight to the top.

17.

BE AWARE OF WHAT YOU DON'T KNOW AND
WHAT YOU'RE NOT GOOD AT

My father used to tell me as he read my poorly written essays in school, "Richard, it's not important that you're not a great speller. It's really important, however, that you know that you're not a good speller. That way, when in doubt, you can use the dictionary." Boy, was he right! I have gotten more mileage out of this tiny piece of wisdom than perhaps any other.

My dad was absolutely correct, but not just about spelling. The same idea applies to virtually everything. In my work, for example, it's not critical that I'm an expert editor as long as I know my own weaknesses and limitations. I can hire someone to fill in where I'm weak. Similarly, I'm not a great coordinator for putting together all the details of a public lecture. No problem. I can hire someone who is. It's always smarter to do this and, in the long run, it's almost always less expensive and more profitable. The only time there would be a problem is if I didn't know that I wasn't good at something or if I was unwilling to admit it.

Chances are you're probably really good at certain things and really bad at others. So what? Why should you frustrate yourself and waste your time doing those things you struggle with? This doesn't mean you can't learn new skills or improve existing ones. It merely suggests that you spend the bulk of your time doing whatever it is you do best as well as that which is most important to your success. It's easy to get bogged down and defeated doing tasks you don't enjoy and aren't very good at. Certainly, many if not most of these tasks need to get done, but not necessarily by you.

What if you could spend an extra two or three hours a day focusing on that which you truly love and are genuinely good at? What would happen to your productivity, creativity, and bottom line? You'll never know for sure until you try, but I can assure you that, for me and for so many others I know, this simple idea has been an extremely profitable insight.

18.

BECOME AWARE OF THE PASSION FACTOR

As Marsha Sinetar's incredible best-seller reminds us, *Do What You Love, the Money Will Follow.* Perhaps the reason this book is so popular is that it reminds us of something we intuitively already know: When we are passionate about what we do, success will follow!

Passion for life and for our work is a critical element of success and abundance. Passion is a virtually unstoppable, attitudinal force that generates energy, creativity, and productivity. When you love what you do, it's difficult not to succeed. Your enthusiasm is obvious to everyone around you and contagious.

Part of the process of creating passion in your work is choosing work that you truly love. Doing so requires conscious choice, which often takes a great deal of courage. It can be frightening to change career directions or to try something new, irrespective of how much we may "want to." After all, most of us were indoctrinated into believing that walking a certain safe path was the way to achieve security.

Fear is a powerful, highly destructive force that prevents many of us from pursuing our dreams. However, if you take a careful look at most successful people, more often than not, they have faced very similar fears and conquered them. A client of mine once said, "I finally asked myself the question, Whose life is this anyway? and when I couldn't answer the question, I knew I had to make a change."

I have a story of my own that reinforces this strategy. Many years ago I was taking the safe route. Shortly after college, I began work for an M.B.A. (master's degree in business). The problem was, I couldn't stand it. I dreaded every class and knew I wasn't on my path, following my own dreams. Although it was extremely frightening to me, I decided to walk out and never return. I was determined to follow my bliss instead of my predetermined career path. It was one of the best, most important decisions of my life.

It's important to ask yourself: How safe is it *really*, spending your time doing something you don't enjoy? How well can you perform a task you dread? How creative and original is your thinking? How easy is it to go the extra mile and/or to do what's necessary to achieve greatness? The answers to each of these questions are clear: Without passion, your odds of success are minimal. You will either struggle in your career or burn out completely. But the opposite is just as true when passion for your work fills your heart. When you follow your heart, when you discover what is truly nourishing to your soul, an abundant, joyful life is just around the corner.

19.

EXPERIMENT WITH THE ONE-HOUR SOLUTION

Today, more than ever before, there are vast numbers of financial opportunities available to those who want one, and who are open-minded to doing something a little different. There are numerous part-time, home-based businesses that are turning ordinary people into millionaires. Many of these businesses are fun, easy, and require no more than a few hours a week. In addition, many of these businesses require very little initial cash to get into and no prior experience.

So what's the catch? Well, there is one, and you have probably already guessed it. As is so often the case, fear and worry are the greatest dream snatchers. The excuses I hear from people range from "I'm afraid I don't have the time " to "I'm afraid I can't do it" to "I'm afraid of what people will think." Fear is the single most self-defeating emotion in our lives.

What would happen if you decided to follow the advice of this book's title, *Don't Worry, Make Money*? As an experiment, I suggest the following strategy. I predict that if you banish worry from your consciousness and choose a credible, financially solid, ethical home-based or multilevel marketing business, you can become financially independent in as little as one hour a day. You don't have to quit your job, change careers, or take on a great deal of risk. Spend some time investigating what's out there. Ask around. Be willing to do something a little different. Keep an open mind. Don't worry!

The only catch is that you must actually spend a full, noninterrupted hour, each and every day, doing what is the critical inch of that business. You must spend the hour without fear! You must not worry about the outcome, about what others are thinking about you, about your past failures, about the fact that you don't have very much time, or about the fact that what you are doing isn't in your nature, or anything else. If the most important part of the business is making phone calls, then you must spend the better part of your hour making those calls. You don't have to spend one minute longer than your agreed-upon hour, but for this experiment to be given a chance, you must give it an honest hour. I predict that if you pick a business that you love, and you faithfully spend your hour doing the key parts of the business (not simply busy work), that within two years you will be well on your way to complete financial independence.

The first and most important step is to eliminate worry from your life. If you choose to experiment with this strategy, I wish you the best of luck. I know you can be as successful as your imagination will allow.

20.

BE PREPARED TO WALK AWAY FROM A
NEGOTIATION—YOU CAN USUALLY GO BACK

Many people get less out of a negotiation than is otherwise possible because of fear—fear that if they don't accept the terms of the deal, as is, they sabotage the deal completely. While it's possible this could occur, it's far more likely that you will sabotage your success—both immediate and long term—if you are unwilling to walk away from a negotiation. If you believe in your product or service, in whatever it is that you bring to the table (your time, your expertise, etc.), you're virtually always better off if you're willing to walk away, to consider the option of starting over or bringing your business elsewhere. This doesn't mean that you *do* walk away; only that you're comfortable doing so. You're not attached, one way or the other.

This don't-worry attitude is applicable in most business situations. Let's consider one of the simplest examples, purchasing a home. Suppose you find a house that you truly love, and the asking price is $100,000. You believe, however, that to make this purchase wisely, you should pay no more than $90,000. The current owner seems stubborn. The problem is, you really love the house and don't want to jeopardize the deal.

Being "attached" to an outcome can cost you a great deal of money. If you feel it's in your best interest to pay no more than $90,000 for this house, the wisest financial and emotional decision you could make would be to offer the $90,000, be willing to walk away, and not worry about it! The simple act of not worrying about the outcome will, more often than not, come back to help you because the truth of the matter is, most people *are* worriers! And it is very likely that the person you are negotiating with is one of them. Although there are rare exceptions, the recipient of your offer will almost never slam the door on the deal at this point. He will, however, be forced into making a very important, quick decision—most likely a decision that *he* is worried about. He can, of course, turn you down, but if he's a worrier, he might not. After all, he's turning away a sure thing in exchange for an unknown future, something that worriers can't stand. He may come back with a counteroffer, but if he knows you're *not* a worrier, that you're perfectly willing to walk away, the counteroffer is likely to be much lower than if he senses your fear. This is pretty simple stuff. But the truth is, the reality of making money and wise decisions isn't very complicated. However, not many people understand the importance of a don't-worry attitude. If you do, you're one step ahead of the game.

A friend of mine is the shrewdest negotiator I have ever seen. He once walked into a car dealership and made an incredibly low-ball offer on a brand-new luxury car. This is exactly what he said: "Good afternoon, sir. I have a certified check in my hands in the amount of $35,250 for which I'd like to buy this particular automobile. I know you're going to have to ask your boss, so the offer is good for nine whole minutes—but not one second longer. I will not pay one penny more for the car, but the check is yours if you want to part with this car." As the visibly nervous salesperson started to respond, my friend calmly looked at his watch and said, "You have eight and one half minutes left before I walk out the door."

He got the car!

Obviously, few of us would have the nerve (or the means) or perhaps even the desire to do this. Yet the example does demonstrate the power of the willingness to walk away. Clearly, my friend's offer had to be in the ballpark for what the car was truly worth. The dealership certainly wasn't going to give the car away. But my friend had factored that into his strategy.

He did some research into the dealer's actual cost, and knew that if they took the deal, they would still make a tiny profit. But he also knew that his price would, in all likelihood, be lower than anyone else had paid for the same car. Since he wanted that particular car but wasn't attached to it, he couldn't lose either way. He knew that, in most cases, a salesman would have to spend a great deal of time with a potential customer before any sale would take place. In this instance, his total time involvement, other than the actual paperwork, was less than nine minutes. It just might be worth it to the dealership to make a quick, small profit rather than wait days, weeks, even months for a larger one. The key was his absolute willingness to walk away with no regrets whatsoever. You can implement this strategy with the utmost respect for the people with whom you are negotiating. There's no need to appear aggressive or obnoxious. All you need is a don't-worry attitude. Experiment with this strategy and, I believe, you will be well rewarded.

21.

BE WILLING TO CHANGE

In his wonderful book *Success Is No Accident,* Dr. Lair Ribeiro makes a statement that rings true to my ears and has been proven repeatedly throughout history. He says, "If you go on doing what you've always done, you'll go on getting what you've always got." What a powerful message! Sometimes, in order to create positive things in your life, you need to make some changes in the way you do things. The world isn't going to suddenly reward you by changing its conditions. Instead, *you* must alter the way you approach certain challenges.

I have met numerous people who are virtually unwilling to change, even when their current efforts aren't working. People are frightened of change. Sometimes they even argue for their limitations by saying things like: "I've always been that way" or "I'm just not that kind of person" or "I've always done it differently." If something *isn't* working for you, however, statements like these aren't relevant or helpful. It's critical to remember that if you go on doing what you've always done, you *will* go on getting what you've always got!

Maybe you're not the type of person who believes in asking friends and family for favors. And you might even be proud of this fact. Still, there are times when asking for help might be just what you need to succeed. If you're stubborn and insist "I can't do that," you may be missing out on a wonderful opportunity. There are countless other examples of where an unwillingness to try something new, or an unwillingness to do something differently, will interfere with your chances for success. Take an inventory of your own stubbornness: Are there areas in your life where you do things a certain way simply because that's the way you've always done them?

Without doubt, "Keep an open mind" is an overused phrase. Yet relatively few of us actually do keep an open mind. Instead, we are stuck in old, worn-out ways. If you drop your fear, and have the courage to be willing to change, my guess is that you won't have to go on much longer getting what you've always had.

22.

SPEND THE BULK OF YOUR TIME ON THE
"CRITICAL INCH" OF YOUR BUSINESS OR PROJECT

Often, the greatest mistake people make in their quest for success is that they focus on the wrong parts of their business. Too much time and energy are spent doing things that, while perhaps necessary, aren't the critical, absolutely important aspects of the business or project. I've seen people frustrated, claiming they "didn't have time" to make the necessary calls, speak to the decision maker, write the offer, ask for the deal, engage in critical due diligence, write the chapter, make the promotional or marketing effort, or whatever else might be the *essential* task—but somehow they did manage to find the time to clean their desk, make a few social calls, organize their computer disks, plan their weekend, review some files, set up a meeting, and do countless other tasks that have limited relevance to performance and success.

Perhaps, at a given moment, solving a particular problem is the "critical inch" of your business; maybe it's generating additional cash flow, diffusing an interpersonal issue with a colleague, finishing a report, writing a speech, or addressing a technical issue. Part of the solution is asking the relevant question: What's truly most important? More often than not, the answer is quite different from the answer to another question: What seems to be the next logical or convenient thing to do? Frequently, we'll jump from one activity to another without any real thought as to the true relevance of our actions. We'll respond to a mini-crisis, phone call, or something that's been sitting on the desk before taking on the one activity that *truly* makes a difference.

About twice a week I work out at a local athletic club. The same principle seems to apply to working out and getting in shape. It's interesting to watch the different ways people "work out." There is one group of people—I'd like to think I'm one of them—who roll up their sleeves and get to work. They go from machine to machine, exercise to exercise, until they have completed their workout. In thirty minutes or less, they can be in the shower and out the door. Generally, these people are in pretty good shape. They did what they intended to do.

There's another group of people, however, who never quite get to it. They socialize a great deal, take fifteen or twenty minutes to get changed, and walk around the gym looking at the equipment. Sometimes they'll read the paper or take a steam bath. Recently, I overheard a phone conversation between one of these men and his wife or girlfriend. He said to her, with a serious look on his face, "Honey, I just don't get it. I come down here to the club virtually every day, but never seem to lose any weight." Now, I've seen this man at the club on many occasions, but I've yet to see him *actually* work out. He's convinced himself that by being there every day, he's doing something worthwhile; yet he's missing the boat entirely. He never seems to do the critical inch—the exercise!

If we're not careful, it's easy to fall into the same basic trap with our business and moneymaking efforts. We may look busy, and do quite a few things during the course of a day, but we might not be focusing on the one or two things that really make a difference. Some of the most successful people I know work only a few hours a day—but boy, do they understand the concept of the critical inch. When you do what's truly necessary and important, the rest seems to fall into place. Take a moment, each day, to reevaluate your priorities. Make sure you spend your time doing that which is going to create success and abundance in your life.

23.

EXPRESS YOUR GRATITUDE TOWARD OTHERS

When it comes right down to it, there are very few sure things in life. Once in a while, however, we come across an idea that is an absolute, always, no matter what, truism. This is one of them, and a good one to remember: *As long as our expression of gratitude is genuine, other people love it and remember it. This not only makes them feel good, but it also encourages them to help us again and to encourage others to do the same.* The people we remember to thank, in person, with a thoughtful note or gesture, or a phone call, are infinitely more likely to help us again than those we take for granted and/or neglect to thank. It's so obvious, yet so few people really understand how this works.

People are inherently good. Most people love helping others, reaching out, lending a hand, offering assistance. For the most part, people love to be remembered or thought of as the person who gave someone else their big break, or some other form of important, loving guidance. The other side of the coin, however, is that people love to be acknowledged, admired, and thanked. People love to be thanked, not out of any selfish need but simply because it feels good to be acknowledged. And when we are sincerely acknowledged, the acknowledgment acts as a reinforcement that we have done the right thing. Thus, we want to do it again. Because people love to reach out to help others—if we thank them for their kindness—it actually nudges them to encourage others to help us, too. Life becomes infinitely easier when we remember to thank others for their acts of kindness.

Many wonderful people have stepped forward to help me in my career and in my life. Whether I have asked for help or received it without request, I always try to remember to express my gratitude. Although I never thank people in order get something in return, I have found that thanking people from the heart guarantees that more help is just around the corner. None of us wants to be taken for granted. We all love to be thanked!

The next time you do something really nice or helpful for someone and they thank you, take note of how it makes you feel. While it's true there are many instances where you would help again without any thanks (those of us who have children know this), I'll bet you'll find yourself even more willing to help someone who expresses their gratitude, which is, of course, also one of the keys to a joyful life. By engaging in constant gratitude, you'll be guaranteeing success, abundance, *and* happiness.

24.

LEAVE A GREAT IMPRESSION
(NOT JUST A GOOD ONE)

I guess you could say that this strategy is the opposite of the "don't burn any bridges" concept. The feeling others have for you can be a critical element of success. In all cases, when people have a nice feeling toward you, it sets you apart and gives you an ethical, well-deserved advantage in all you do. This doesn't mean you should pretend to be someone you're not, only that you recognize that your presence, behavior, integrity, and kindness will leave a lasting imprint in the minds of those you are with.

I once heard an audiotape from Ken Blanchard called "Raving Fans." In it, he described the importance of setting yourself apart by creating customers who don't simply like your product or service but actually "rave" about it—and you. This strategy is the interpersonal version of creating raving fans. When people think of you, you want them to genuinely want to do business, spend time with, help you. You want your customers, clients, coworkers, colleagues, even competitors, to think and speak highly of you to others.

The way to do this is very simple: Make living your life with absolute integrity and kindness your first priority. Put others first, whenever possible. Be genuinely interested in the lives of other people. Be very present moment oriented with others. Look them in the eye and really focus on what they're saying. Care about them as individuals. Ask about their families. Listen, listen, listen. Finally, make your actions match your good intentions. Stand out from the crowd. Be the one to thank your customers and the people with whom you work. Send a card or thoughtful note, even flowers if it's appropriate. Make people remember you in a positive light.

If you implement this strategy with your own unique touches and if you are genuine in your thoughts and actions, you will create, over time, a stellar, "one in a million" reputation with virtually everyone you come in contact with. People will be beating down your door for the opportunity to work with or even to spend time with you. What's more, your life will be filled with more joy and loving kindness than you ever thought possible.

25.

MAINTAIN WEALTH CONSCIOUSNESS

Developing wealth consciousness is what this book is all about. Wealth consciousness suggests a complete absence of money worries; an awareness that there is always plenty of money to go around. People who live with true abundance never worry about having enough—they know that creating wealth and affluence is a function of their own mind-set. Worry keeps us from feeling free and joyful. We are never truly free until we break the chains of fear. But once we do, our lives will never be the same. A life without worry is a life of abundance, a life well lived.

That which we focus our attention on expands. If we spend our mental energy worrying, it's difficult if not impossible to create great abundance. Our fear gets in the way of our creativity and traps us in the status quo. In other words, our fear "interferes" with our means of creation. On the other hand, if we are free of worries, if we maintain wealth consciousness, money will flow to us in inexhaustible ways. We will literally create ways to keep money flowing in our direction. Our antennas will be on the lookout for new and exciting opportunities, and our minds will be open to embrace them.

The most important point about wealth consciousness can be summed up with the adage, "Don't put the cart before the horse." Make no mistake about it: Wealth consciousness comes first! You will not suddenly develop wealth consciousness if and when you become "wealthy." It's the other way around. You develop wealth consciousness by eliminating worry, by trusting in the universe and in your own inner resources. Once you secure your wealth consciousness, true abundance is just around the corner.

26.

WAIT FOR INSPIRATION

Ironically, it's often the case that the best use of our time is to do absolutely nothing—to not act, to simply wait for an answer. But in our speeded up, frentic culture, most of us panic if we aren't actively doing something, even if that "something" isn't wise, productive, or useful. Most of us are so busy, or at least looking busy, that we can't see or hear our own wisdom.

Built into our psyche is a wealth of wisdom. We all have innate common sense at our disposal that can provide us with solutions, inspiration, and guidance. The problem is, we must quiet down enough to hear it. We must wait for inspiration.

To access our innate health takes some humility and getting used to. We must be willing to admit that "we don't know what to do" at a given moment. We must learn to be a little patient; it's worth the wait. The simple act of admitting that you *don't know* an answer, at present, activates your inner wisdom and guidance. By simply being willing to wait for inspiration, you virtually guarantee that it will come—in most cases, rather quickly. Not always, but sometimes, your mind needs a few minutes, occasionally longer, to cultivate the most appropriate answer. The answers you receive, however, will surprise and delight you. Your thinking and instincts will rise to a new level.

27.

USE THE POWER OF REFLECTION

Reflection is one of the most underused yet powerful tools for success. It is a passive way to pinpoint solutions and strategies with the least amount of effort or wasted energy. It's the opposite of "trying too hard," of forcing an answer. Reflection is more a matter of allowing an answer to unfold right before your eyes, often with little or no effort on your part.

One of the benefits of reflection is that it enables us to get our egos out of the way. In a quiet state of mind we are able to see things clearly, including our own contributions to problems, new ways of doing things, and the ways we get in our own way. Reflection allows us to sense our self-imposed limitations and some of the blind spots in our thinking.

Reflection is simply a matter of getting out of your own way. It's about quieting down your mind so that answers can arise within the quietness. Often, when we're looking for an answer, we "turn up the volume" of our thinking. This might be called active problem solving. We think, think, think—and then we think some more. We get personally involved in the process. We take the credit for finding solutions and the blame when we cannot. For the most part, when we are actively thinking, we're thinking about that which we already know, that with which we are familiar. We try to solve a problem at the same level of understanding that initially created it. And often we go around in circles.

People who regularly use reflection, on the other hand, understand that we are connected to, and a part of, a deeper intelligence. This quiet source of wisdom is available to all of us in unlimited doses because it is always present. The only factor preventing us from hearing or being connected to this wisdom is the noise or chatter of our own thinking. When we turn the "volume" of our thinking down, we can begin to sense this deeper intelligence. This is reflection.

Recently I was engaged in an interpersonal conflict with someone I was working with. In my mind, I was blaming him for virtually all of our problems. The more I thought about it, the more convinced I was that the problem was him. It got so bad that I considered breaking up the partnership, which, to that point, had been very successful. My wife, Kris, suggested I stop thinking about it entirely and postpone making any decisions. She suggested instead that I take a drive and spend some time in quiet reflection. I took her advice. As I quieted down, it became clear to me that a great deal of our problems were actually coming from me. I could see how I was contributing to our poor communication and unrealistic expectations.

You may be shocked at how easily most problems can be solved when you simply step out of the way by quieting down. You may also be pleasantly surprised at the ease with which new and creative ideas will flow into your life. Although your mind will be quiet, it won't be turned off. Instead, you will be using a new part of your mind—a softer, wiser part—that understands the path of least resistance and the source of new answers. Success is often a function of doing something exceptionally well or more creatively than it has been done before. Reflection is a powerful vehicle to bring this about.

28.

LAUGH AT YOUR MISTAKES

(AND YOU WON'T REPEAT THEM)

Have you ever noticed that the more seriously you take your mistakes, the more you make them? And the more seriously you take your problems, the more you create them? This is because your behavior follows your attention just as surely as baby puppies follow their mother. Wherever the bulk of your energy lies, your behavior is sure to follow. When your mind is full of confusing or conflicting details, mistakes, and problems, your attention is riveted in a negative direction. Thus, when you make a big deal out of something you have done wrong, when you take yourself too seriously, you are actually setting the stage to repeat the mistake.

Mental energy is a very powerful and potentially useful tool. However, energy cuts both ways. If your energy is directed exclusively toward problems and concerns, that is what you will see and what you will tend to create. If your energy is abundant, however, your mind will be in a more creative mode—searching for solutions, seeing opportunities, building on strengths. Your mind will be open to suggestions to new and better ways of doing things. You will have a winning attitude.

In terms of expending energy, it is far more powerful to be in favor of something positive than to be against something negative—*for* peace instead of against violence, *for* excellence instead of against mediocrity.

A decision to make light of your mistakes, to remain lighthearted, doesn't mean you don't care or that you're not concerned with making an error. It simply means that you refuse to compound a problem by making a bigger deal out of something than is absolutely necessary. It means that you understand the value of keeping your perspective and sense of humor even in the face of adversity.

In every mistake there is the potential for growth. Inherent in every problem there is a solution. When you take the process too seriously, however, you interfere with your ability to see answers. The next time you make a mistake, instead of dealing with it in your usual way, chuckle at yourself instead. You will be surprised at how quickly and easily you are able to resolve the issue.

29.

TAKE YOUR LUNCH

Although you or the person you live with might worry about the effort or time it takes to prepare a lunch, there are some potentially valuable benefits in doing so. Consider this: Suggest to one or more of your friends at work that you would like to do an experiment for a couple of days. The experiment would be that you each bring your lunch and, depending on weather and other factors, plan to go to a nearby park, lake, hilltop, or some other interesting setting to eat it.

The idea is to then combine the lunch group with an investment club where you exchange ideas and investment options. Depending on the structure of the group, members can take turns bringing special food items. Not only can this be a great deal of fun and a lot healthier than eating at a restaurant, but enormously profitable as well. For example, if you stayed on the job for thirty years and substituted a $2 lunch for a $7.50 lunch at a local restaurant, the $5.50-per-day savings deposited in an investment club earning 8 percent over thirty years would amount to around $100,000. And those of us who eat at restaurants frequently know these numbers are extremely conservative.

Even if your investment club met only two or three times per week, the door would be open for some new, "worry-free" ways to create wealth. One of the goals in creating your "club" is to create the discipline and mind-set for regular investing. Once you are thinking in terms of investing instead of spending, you can duplicate this process in other areas. A small bonus from your employer, for example, can be spent on consumer items, *or* it can be invested in your new account to make it grow. The same is true with a tax refund, a surprise gift from a relative, even accumulated

67

pocket change. Anytime you come across a little extra money you may find yourself investing in your future. Over time, your earnings can be extraordinary.

Once you have established this type of wealth-building mind-set, the benefits will continue to grow. You will find yourself making different types of financial decisions that pay off in really big ways. You may decide to buy term insurance instead of whole life and, unlike so many others, you will actually invest the difference! You may choose a more affordable automobile and, rather than feeling deprived, actually feel excited that you get to invest the difference in yourself. You'll discover that investing in this manner is a great deal of fun. Rather than worrying about your future, you'll be making joyful choices to secure a worry-free life. Who would believe that bringing your lunch to work could be such a profitable thing to do?

30.

ASK FOR WHAT YOU WANT

Jack Canfield and Mark Victor Hansen, authors of *Chicken Soup for the Soul*, call this simple strategy "The Aladdin Factor." It's astonishing what you can accomplish by simply asking for what you want—help, a raise, forgiveness, an idea, another chance, a break, or whatever. And not only can you get what you want by asking for it, but often the person you are asking will thank you for taking the initiative.

If it's so obviously helpful and important to ask for what we want, why do so few of us do it? Once again, the answer is fear. We worry about the outcome. We're afraid of rejection or a negative response. We might be worried about offending someone or being perceived of as weak, or of taking advantage of our relationship. We may feel we don't deserve help. For a multitude of reasons, we allow past negative experiences and/or our own made-up fears to taint our present opportunities.

Several years ago I had the realization that one of my own greatest assets was *my* willingness to help others. Hundreds of times, I've returned calls to complete strangers, or written a response to one of their questions. With friends and family, my willingness to help is even greater. Whenever possible, within reason, I'm there to help. I realized that helping others, offering assistance, doing favors, feeling needed and wanted is a deep and important human need. It feels wonderful to be needed.

This being the case, I realized that, for the most part, other people feel the same way. Despite our fears and concerns to the contrary, it's actually quite arrogant and self-righteous to assume that others aren't as willing to help. I'm not the only nice guy around. What in the world was I thinking? The key in asking for something, large or small, is to be sincere in your belief that, deep down, others *want* to help you. You must approach your request by assuming that the person you are asking is just like you—he or she has an inner longing to be of help.

This simple insight about the goodwill of others dramatically speeded up my path to success—as it will yours. It meant that I no longer had to do everything myself. I didn't have to develop all my ideas and projects on my own. There were plenty of others more than willing to pitch in and offer their expertise, assistance, and advice. Today, when I ask someone to sit down with me and share an idea, it often sparks ideas that help them as well. What goes around comes around. Those who are willing to help others are always paid back in one way or another. Obviously, this isn't a prescription to run out and take advantage of people. To think in these terms would be to miss the whole point of this strategy. Your own good judgment will prevent you from doing this. Once you remove the fear of asking for help, your wisdom and common sense will instruct you when and how to ask.

Rather than being afraid to ask for help, remember this: When you ask someone to help you, you are actually doing *them* a tremendous favor by giving them an opportunity to feel needed. Beginning today, rub your magic lamp and experiment with "The Aladdin Factor."

31.

SHORT CIRCUIT YOUR REACTION SPIRALS

It's a rare person who can avoid the trap of reaction spirals. This is the insidious tendency to overreact to something—and then compound the problem by overanalyzing it. Here is a typical example: Someone criticizes some aspect of your work. You overreact to the criticism and become defensive. As if that weren't bad enough, you spend the next half hour analyzing the critical comments, convincing yourself they are incorrect. A whirlwind of thoughts pass through your mind. You focus on them. The more you do, the worse you feel, and the more tired you become.

The question is, how effective are you when you're feeling overwhelmed, defensive, and stubborn? The truth is, in a negative state of mind, we expend unnecessary energy, make very poor decisions, and lose our creativity and sense of joy. Wouldn't it be wonderful if you could nip these reaction spirals in the bud?

You can! The trick is to see them coming and to commit, in advance, to "short circuiting" them. With every negative reaction comes a negative feeling—a feeling of irritation, annoyance, or impatience. We often use these feelings to justify further negativity. For example, we say to ourselves something like, "I have a right to be angry." Now that we're focused on our anger, we think about other instances that make us angry, and so on. This fuels our negative feelings and creates a negative spiral.

If, instead of compounding our negative feelings, we used them as a signal to alert us to potential trouble, we would be in a much better position to stop the cycle before it got out of hand. The other day, for example, I was waiting for an important phone call. I waited and waited. In my mind,

I was certain that the person I was waiting for had agreed to call me at a certain time on a specific phone line. I had canceled other plans to make time for her. Her understanding, however, was that I was to call her. Because I was on the other line while waiting for her call, I didn't phone her either. Finally, she called. And when she did, she was extremely angry at me. Instantly, I became defensive and angry. "How dare she?" I thought to myself. I was enraged. What saved me was my ability to use my negative feelings as an protective alarm! Like a flashing light, I was reminded to calm down, which allowed me to see our mutual innocence. One of us had made a mistake. Big deal. Moments after I became angry, a little voice inside my head said, "Relax. Don't turn this into a big deal." Within a few moments, I regained my perspective and simply apologized. Honestly, I have no way of knowing who was at fault. And who cares? The point is, had I continued in my reaction spiral I would have clearly jeopardized my working relationship with this person. As it turned out, our little misunderstanding was a nonissue. We both were able to get past it in a matter of seconds. No wasted energy, no heated debate, no unnecessary discussion, no defensive or passive-aggressive behavior.

Many potential problems can be averted with this simple strategy. All you really need is the wisdom to understand that negative reactions aren't in your best interest, and the humility and willingness to back off and start over. Abundance is a joyful path. Occasionally, however, we lose our way. Don't waste your precious energy compounding an already negative situation. You'll be amazed how much smoother your life will become and how easily you can get back on track when you short circuit your reaction spirals.

32.

ELIMINATE YOUR MOST SELF-DEFEATING BELIEF

All of us have beliefs that get in our way. And for many of us, there is one in particular—some nagging, habitual tenet that we have come to accept as "just the way things are." For me, it was my belief that "I don't have enough time." Day after day, for most of my adult life, I would remind myself of this limiting concept. Sometimes I would tell myself this many times in a single day.

What possible value could there be in telling yourself this—or any—self-created negative belief? Consider the subtle messages that go along with this idea. After all, if I believe that "I don't have enough time," I must also believe that "I'll never get something done on time," "I'll be under constant pressure," "There's no time to lose," as well as other related, limiting ideas that directly interfere with my success and quality of life. Does this belief help me get things done? Of course not! Does it bring me joy? No. Any effect this belief has is strictly negative.

What's *your* most self-defeating belief? Is it that you believe you aren't good enough, or lucky enough? Maybe you believe you don't deserve success, or that other people control your destiny. Perhaps you believe that people are out to get you, or that you are a victim of circumstance. Whatever it is, it's not worth keeping and it's certainly not worth defending! But each time you remind yourself—by telling yourself—of your limiting belief, you are reinforcing an idea that directly interferes with your own success. It puts a wall between where you are and where you want to be. Each time you say to yourself, "I never get any breaks," or "I can't help it, I've always been that way," or whatever negative message you are sending, it's as if you are saying to yourself, "I don't want to succeed."

73

Each time I slip into my old habit of telling myself that I don't have enough time, I keep in mind the damage I am inflicting on myself. I remind myself that there is zero value in this, or any, self-defeating belief. I suggest you do the same thing. You may be surprised, even shocked, at how often you repeat self-defeating statements to yourself and/or to others. The good news is that you'll be pleasantly surprised at how easily you can rid yourself of their negative effects. Simply refuse to continue. Make a commitment to yourself to stop reinforcing this—and all—negative beliefs by discussing them, or even thinking about them. As familiar negativity comes to mind, gently dismiss it as you would flies at a picnic. Don't give it your valuable attention. Save your energy for positive ideas and action. Once you get your most self-defeating ideas out of the way, you'll discover that abundance and joy will be right around the corner.

33.

KEEP IN MIND THAT CIRCUMSTANCES DON'T
MAKE A PERSON, THEY REVEAL HIM

It's extremely rare to find a successful person who whines, complains, and frets about her circumstances. This is despite the fact that she may have overcome great obstacles to achieve her level of success. On the other hand, it's extremely common for struggling individuals to continually blame their circumstances for their lack of joy and abundance. The real question is: What came first—the attitude or the success? The answer, in virtually all cases, is that the winning, positive attitude came first, followed by a lifetime of abundance.

Your circumstances are what they are; they were what they were. If you are forty-five years old and were a middle child, you're still going to be a middle child when you're ninety-five. If you're black or white; a woman or a man; or if you were abused, taken advantage of, or bankrupt—these facts cannot change. If your parents couldn't afford to send you to college or if you had to work your way through school, shovel snow in your driveway, or walk ten miles to school—these are all things in your past. It's time to get over them and move on.

You'll find that life will be a lot easier and much more fun when you make the decision to drop your complaining. All it does is make you feel sorry for yourself—sad, angry, victimized, suspicious, and/or self-righteous. When you argue for your limitations, your thoughts and words merely get in your way and greatly interfere with your ability to create. With complaining out of the way, you'll create the space for an explosion of creativity and brilliance. You'll be able to be more focused and oriented to the present moment. Instead of focusing on problems, you'll begin to see solutions. Instead of maintaining an "I can't" attitude, you'll quickly develop a more positive vision for yourself.

All it takes is a simple decision; the decision to stop yourself from falling into the complaining habit. At first it may be difficult—even funny—to observe how often you complain. Habits can be hard to break. But in this case, it's well worth the effort. As an excuse or complaint comes to mind, gently shoo it away like you would flies at a picnic. Don't worry about it too much. You'll quickly get used to the nicer feelings that come from a life without complaints, as well as the success that comes with your new winning attitude!

34.

FORM A WINNING PARTNERSHIP

As you probably already know, the wrong partnership—professional or personal—can be far worse than no partnership. And a winning partnership can be worth its weight in gold. Sometimes, however, fear can keep us from seeking out good partners and forming winning partnerships. Many people worry that they will have to share the profits, decision-making authority, and/or prestige that come with a project or business. A fearful attitude, of course, won't allow us to do this. As always, it's a good idea to overcome this fear so that you will know whether forming a winning partnership is in your best interest.

There are a few important points to consider when deciding if a partnership is right for you. If the members of a partnership do essentially the same thing, it's almost inevitable that one will be harder working and have more commitment than the other. Often, that partner begins to resent pulling the other partner along. Likewise, the partner being pulled resents the other partner's pushing. It's generally *not* a winning partnership. For example, two trial attorneys go into a legal partnership. At the end of the year, one or the other might wonder what benefit he received from the partnership. After all, each is fully capable of doing the other's job. But, if a trial attorney and a corporate attorney go into partnership, usually each one, at the end of the year says, "Thank God for my partner—I don't know what I would do without him."

Ideally, each partner brings to the table different skills and attributes. One might be excellent at details and planning, the other in promotion and public speaking. Or one might be excellent in sales, the other in marketing. A good partnership is like a good marriage—it has to be formed carefully. If you can create the right combination of skills, work ethic, and vision you can create a winning team.

Here's a classic example of a winning partnership. Alan and George each had poor financial years the past few years. Alan is a superb real estate deal maker and has an artistic flair. Although he could negotiate to purchase building lots and negotiate to sell, he did not have any serious product or any true expertise in building custom homes. George is a superior tradesman and building contractor, but he had been working only about half-time. He didn't have the foresight to locate great building sites or the courage to be a tough negotiator. They formed a partnership. Right from the start, their partnership was a match made in heaven. In their very first year of working together, they *each* had their most successful year ever. It's true that they had to split their profits, but their combination of skills *quadrupled* their ability to produce. The key is that the partnership does something that neither could do by themselves. Now, George is busy full-time building custom homes, the thing he does best. Alan is busy negotiating to purchase lots for future building, working on design, subcontracting, and negotiating material pricing. Although it sounds unbelievable, the partnership is able to complete a beautiful custom home, start to finish, in a matter of a few months. This is a winning partnership.

You may be the most talented person on earth, but until you hook up with a good partner, you may never truly unleash that talent. Rather than spending your energy trying to do everything, you and your new partner can each focus on what she or he does best.

35.

LET GO OF FEARFUL THOUGHTS

If you gathered up all the fearful thoughts that exist in the mind of the average person, looked at them objectively, and tried to decide just how much good they provided that person, you would see that not some but all fearful thoughts are useless. They do no good. Zero. They interfere with dreams, hopes, desires, and progress.

Fearful thoughts take many different forms. Sometimes they sound reasonable: "I'm just being careful, so I'm taking my time." Other times they are tied to your past: "I've tried that before and it didn't work." Occasionally, fears are cleverly disguised as being realistic: "Most people fail, so I want to be absolutely sure before I get started." I could fill page after page with other examples. Yet when you take a close, honest look at every fearful thought, there are threads of similarity. All of them are explanations or rationalizations for why something shouldn't or can't work. They are usually justifications for quitting, or for not getting started. To me, fearful thoughts are like a leash on an energetic dog. They hold you back, not some but all of the time.

A critic, especially a fearful one, will look at this advice and say it's unrealistic, simplistic, and/or foolish. The problem with overcoming these objections is that, on the surface, they sound reasonable. Let me assure you that I'm not suggesting you ignore the facts and take unnecessary and/or foolish risks. Nor am I suggesting that you should attempt things you are totally unqualified for. For example, if your dream is to play basketball in the NBA and you're forty-five years old, overweight, and five feet six inches tall, forget it. You're not going to make it!

What I'm talking about here are the fears that clearly and directly interfere with your dreams—the fear of rejection, the fear of failure; thoughts like "What will everyone think of me? I might look foolish," or "I don't think I can do it, I don't have the time, or the experience, or the confidence, or the budget." These common, ongoing fearful thoughts are the dream snatchers of our own making.

For example, I know a person who was working as an independent salesperson. Her goal was to double her income. Her "rational" fear played itself out like this: "I can't call people on the weekends because I might offend them or take away from their family time." The truth, of course, was that she was frightened to make the calls. So, for years and years, she didn't make the calls and she always fell far short of her goals. Then one day she decided to simply drop her fear and pick up the phone. Because more of her clients were home and tended to be more relaxed on the weekends, she discovered that it was the best possible time to call. Once she dropped her fear, it was easy. Her income didn't double, it tripled.

At the risk of being overly simplistic, let me suggest you try something that can change your life. Make a commitment that, for the next month, you will practice dropping and/or ignoring any negative and fearful thought that enters your mind. As fears come to your mind, gently but firmly let them go. As they return (which they will), let them go again. It's easier than you think. It just takes courage and a little practice. Do this again and again until they disappear completely. You'll discover that life is so much easier and more fun without the interference of fearful thoughts.

36.

THINK BIG!

The implications of thinking big are widespread and impressive. Thinking big is a magic door opener that broadens your perspective and allows you to see new opportunities. Thinking big makes life easier and a lot more fun. It also makes large profits more probable.

I've been repeatedly reminded by successful businesspeople in virtually every field that thinking big is one of the keys to success. Let's consider a few examples. Successful insurance salespersons insist that it takes the *identical* amount of time to speak to someone about a million-dollar policy as it does a one-thousand-dollar policy. In the real estate field, the concept of leverage applies whether you're considering a single-family home or a huge apartment building. This doesn't mean that you can't make money in single-family homes, or that your rate of return will necessarily be higher with more expensive properties. It merely suggests that the bigger your vision, the larger your potential for success. If you're trying to sell homes for a living, as an agent, it takes the same amount of energy to ask a wealthy person for their listing as it does a low-end homeowner. You can think small, or you can think big.

In any field where public speaking is in order, this concept is critical. It takes an hour to speak to a single person and the same sixty minutes to speak to a crowd of one thousand or more. The size of your crowd will be affected by the size of your vision. The concept of thinking big also applies to whom you choose to talk to. Are you frightened to go to the top? If so, you're missing out. It's very often the case that the people highest up the ladder are actually the easiest to speak to—and the most willing to help. I've had the owners of car dealerships actually sit in the car and give me a test drive at the same dealership where the salesperson on the floor wouldn't give me the time of day. But in order to make that happen, I had to ask. In the corporate world, the boss is often more than willing to sit down with you, even when middle-level managers treat you with disrespect. It's a strange dynamic, but it's often true.

As usual, the primary reason many people think too small is fear. Thoughts like, "I can't speak to a room full of people," "I can't risk taking on a larger project," and "I couldn't ask the boss to have lunch with me" fill the mind and are taken too seriously. When fearful thoughts enter the mind, try to banish them. You can do it—once you believe you can. The fear you are experiencing is almost always self-created and usually unnecessary.

I have a friend who spent most of his adult life insisting he couldn't write a book. This was very puzzling to me, because not only was he an excellent writer, but he also felt quite comfortable writing articles and chapters! One day I asked him to consider the idea that a book is nothing more than a series of interesting chapters put into sequence. As obvious as this was to me, he had never thought of it in those terms. Instead, he had always focused on his stubborn belief that writing a book was too big a project. This simple shift in his thinking made all the difference. Two years later, he finished his first book.

Take a look at your own vision for abundance. Is your vision too small? Could you be thinking in larger terms? In most cases, the answer is yes! There may be ways that you can reach more people with the same amount of effort. Regardless of the business you are in, the first step is to eliminate any fear or worry that is getting in your way. As your worrisome thoughts gradually disappear and become less appealing, new ideas and insights will begin to emerge.

An acquaintance of mine operates a coffeehouse. For years she did everything herself. She didn't hire a staff because she was concerned that she couldn't afford to expand. The problem was, because she had to do everything herself, her service was rather slow. It hadn't occurred to her that she was losing a great deal of business because of her growing reputation for being slow. She knew that something was wrong, and that people waiting for their morning coffee didn't want to stand in long lines. One day she asked herself, "If I wasn't fearful, what would I do?" The answer was obvious: "I'd hire a few kids to speed up my service." To her absolute delight, this was the answer to her dreams. Her lines speeded up and her profits soared. As is usually the case, there was really nothing to fear—it was all in her mind. Don't worry, make money!

37.

MAKE DECISIONS WITH THE ADVANTAGE OF *LONG-TERM* INFORMATION INSTEAD OF THE DISADVANTAGE OF *SHORT-TERM* INFORMATION

Oh, how tempting it can be to reverse this bit of wisdom and act on impulse. For example, if you looked only at 1996 when the Dow Jones average grew at a 26 percent rate, based on that short-term bit of information, you might be tempted to sell everything you own and invest in nothing other than the stock market! If so, you could always have the experience of a major downward correction over the short term. Or, if you looked at the rates of return that investors were enjoying in the California residential real estate market in the mid-1980s, you may have been tempted to do the same with single-family homes. If you did so, however, and stayed in the game too long, you would have been brought back to earth—perhaps even made homeless—by the end of the decade! You can see that acting on impulse—or on short-term information alone— can be a big mistake.

Instead, make the bulk of your decisions with the advantage of long-term information instead of the disadvantage of short-term information. This wiser way of approaching your decisions gives you a far more realistic outlook. It also takes most of the worry out of investing and business decisions. For example, if you take *any* twenty-year period of time (excluding the disaster of the 1930s), such as the last twenty years, the rate of return in the market was somewhere in the neighborhood of 10 to 15 percent, depending on what particular index or group of stocks you selected. You can be fairly certain that, within reason, this trend will continue.

38.

KNOW WHEN TO BET, WHEN TO HOLD,
AND WHEN TO FOLD

Many people fail to recognize just how important timing really is. Not just the type of timing we usually think of—catching the stock market or a real estate cycle at precisely the right time—but rather the ongoing inner calculations of knowing when to bet, when to stay put, and when to fold or give something up entirely.

Often, the worst (or at least the most unnecessary) thing you can do in a moneymaking venture is to take a significant risk at the wrong time. Or, on the other end of the risk-taking spectrum, to be overly conservative when it's absolutely appropriate to expand, when the wind seems to be at your back, when a certain degree of risk is in order.

There are times when the best possible course of action is to do nothing other than hold on, do essentially nothing, be patient. Other times, of course, it's important or at least appropriate to expand, to grow, to move forward. Occasionally, you're in the "zone"; everything you touch, every decision you make, seems to turns to gold or take you in a positive direction. Other times we can save ourselves a fortune, or a great deal of energy, by simply being willing to take a loss now, to fold, rather than lose everything later.

It's amazing how often problems can be overcome and new opportunities can be realized by simply quieting down "the inner chatter" of our analytical thinking so that we'll know what action (if any) to take. This quieting of the mind allows us to get out of our own way so that we can know how to put the odds in our favor.

Wisdom is knowing when to do what. It's about being flexible and being willing to change, to flow. And while this may sound obvious, many people make the wrong choices simply because their mind is too busy. Thus, they fall into bad habits and are unwilling to consider new ways of thinking—"I've always done it that way" or "I can't close down this office, we've been here for two generations."

My suggestion here is to simply quiet down enough to consider the facts. Sometimes, a nonreturned phone call can cost you a career, a big deal, or a great deal of money. Other times, it's absolutely appropriate to avoid returning a phone call—it can actually be a good idea. The trick is to act from a place of wisdom rather than simply reacting out of habit.

39.

CHANGE WHAT YOU CAN,
ACCEPT THE THINGS YOU CAN'T

This strategy is adopted from the serenity prayer that says, in its entirety: "Lord, grant me the strength to change the things I can, the serenity to accept the things I cannot, and the wisdom to know the difference." What an incredibly powerful message! Can you imagine how smoothly your life would run if you could implement this strategy most of the time?

In every business there are things we *must* deal with. There are things we can change, that we have some power to control. There are other things that are absolutely beyond our control. Yet how often do we spend our time and energy doing absolutely nothing about the things we do have some control over, while whining and complaining about those things we can't do anything about? Often, because we have our priorities twisted in the wrong direction, we end up chasing our tails and wasting time. Once we change gears, put these factors into proper perspective, and focus only on those things that we have some capacity to control, it's easy to get back on track.

A friend of mine recently retired from an extremely successful career in the real estate syndication business. He insists that many of his competitors failed, in part, because of their lack of acceptance of the "way things really are." Instead of focusing on what they could and should have been doing, many people spent their time complaining about bureaucracy and trying to get around the rules and regulations. In his words, "Dealing with bureaucracy is a part of the business. The Securities and Exchange Commission and other government agencies are just part of the game. If you moan, bitch, and complain, you're sunk!" Similarly, builders *must* deal with permits, government agencies, and environmental and safety factors. Farmers must deal with weather conditions and other factors beyond their control. Corporate people must deal with ridiculous memos, interminable meetings, and bad bosses. Inevitably, the most successful people in any field are those who dance with the "what is" part of business instead of struggling against it. Those who fail are often the ones who struggle against the inevitable.

It's tempting to focus on aspects of life that are beyond our control. How often do you hear people complaining about taxes? While no one (myself included) *likes* to pay taxes, and certainly no one should pay any more than he or she is legally required to pay, there is a great deal of wisdom in spending your time creating abundance rather than complaining about taxes.

Go ahead and lobby for lower taxes if you must. Voice your opinion if you choose to do so. But once you have done what you *can* do, let go of it. Know when to quit. Expend your energy doing what you can do— focus on creation, creativity, positive ideas, and solutions. Come up with a new idea—a useful product or service, or a new or improved way of doing something. Improve your existing business, formulate a new relationship, make a phone call you've been avoiding. Stop complaining about taxes; focus, instead, on making so much money that taxes will seem irrelevant! Do something positive, something you have control over. Once you start thinking in these terms, you'll be amazed at how easy and enjoyable it is to create the abundance you desire and deserve.

40.

DEVELOP RELATIONSHIPS WITH PEOPLE BEFORE
YOU NEED SOMETHING FROM THEM

So many of us wait until we desperately need something from someone before we take the time to get to know them. In truth, this is probably the absolute worst time to do so. If you need something from someone and they know it, they may be on guard, even defensive, trying to determine if you are sincere. The truth is, people are so much more pleasant when you don't need anything from them.

How many people have taken the time to actually sit down, or have coffee with, the manager at their bank (before ever needing a loan)? As a percentage, virtually no one does this. Yet how much easier it is to work with people when they already know and trust you, when you know the names of their spouse and children, when they know that you care about their happiness and that you are a sincere, trusting person.

I make it a point to get to know as many people as possible in my own community. I'm friendly with the banker, the owners of the restaurants and coffee shops, the local mechanic, the pharmacist, the florist, and so many others. The result is that, if I need a loan, my banker knows my face and my name. He trusts me. If I wanted one, he'd probably give me a loan over the phone! If one of my children is sick, the local pharmacist will gladly take the time to discuss the issue with me. He's genuinely concerned about my family as I am about his. If I want to send someone flowers, I can call the florist and say, "Can you make this order extra special?" In every case, she'll go out of her way to please me because she knows I care about her. If I have friends in town and want a great seat at the restaurant, my waiter friend at the diner is more than willing to save me a great table.

This has nothing to do with taking advantage of people. It's just the way life works. People love to help those they know and trust. Each of these people, and so many others, know that I'll do (and have done) special things for them as well. In fact, I wouldn't think twice about it.

Although people will do so, no one *really* wants to get to know you—to be the recipient of your kindness—only during those occasions when you need something from them. It can seem disingenuous, as if you're only being nice because you want something. Of course, it's better that you're friendly now than never, but how much nicer it is if the people you need already know that you're a nice, genuine person. Why not show people how wonderful you are, right now?

Obviously, there are some instances when you will need to meet someone under less than optimal circumstances—and you will need something from them. For example, if your car breaks down, you probably won't know the tow-truck driver. In these instances, make the best of it and leave a great impression. But whenever possible, try to meet and enjoy people before you need them. You'll be shocked at how helpful they can be.

41.

BE AWARE OF YOUR UNIQUE "STACKING ORDER"

The idea of a stacking order was introduced to me by a successful computer consultant. What a gift it has turned out to be! Essentially, the concept exists to help you clarify, in your own mind, how much work, or how many projects you are comfortable working on at any given time.

Over and over again, I've seen incredibly competent people failing simply because they—or their employer—haven't taken this concept into serious consideration.

Everyone is different. We each have different strengths and weaknesses. But, beyond this, we have very unique temperaments regarding an optimal pace to work, how much we can handle, how much is "on our plate," or how many projects we can manage, at any given time.

An area where many people can relate to this concept is in their personal reading habits. Some people love to read one book at a time. They enjoy each page, and won't even think of picking up another until they are completely finished. Other people are just the opposite. They love to have five or six books going at once. They will read a chapter or two in one book, put it down, and perhaps not pick it up again for several weeks. If you forced people to ignore their reading preference (their stacking order), you would take them out of their natural rhythm and ruin their experience of reading. Their comprehension would decrease and their enjoyment level would diminish.

Our work life is very similar, although most people never even consider it to be a factor. Instead, most of us operate as if everyone should work at the same pace and as if we should, or have to, work at someone else's level of activity.

My own preferred "stacking order" is three to four projects at once. This means that I'm most comfortable working on a book, perhaps promoting another one, writing an article, and giving a few lectures a month. If I'm only working on one project, it's simply not enough to keep me engaged. I lose focus, I get a little bored and impatient, and the project doesn't turn out as well as I would like. I love to work a few hours on one project, then shift gears altogether. This may not be the right way to do it, but it's my way. Many people think I'm nuts. I've heard so many people say over the years, "How can you produce so many projects?" The reason it seems nuts to someone else is that their stacking order is different. If I attempted to do it their way, *I'd* go nuts!

Other people love to work on only one project at a time. They focus beautifully on whatever they are working on until they are completely finished. Then, and only then, will they pick up something else. If these people have too many things going at once, they fall apart and look incompetent. It's a shame, because a vast majority of these people are far from incompetent. In fact, in many instances, if these folks were to do nothing other than shift the number of things they focused on at once (i.e., thinking of one or two things or problems or projects, instead of ten) they would begin to look like a genius.

Obviously, there are times when you simply can't work at your preferred pace. You may prefer to work on one project at a time, but be forced by circumstance to work on six or seven. Yet even in these cases, understanding your stacking order can be enormously helpful. You can organize your work in such a way that you can maximize your potential. You can create artificial "time zones" for each of them. For example, you can work on one project for thirty minutes without thinking about anything else whatsoever. Then, after a five-minute break, begin work on project number two. Rather than jumping back and forth, stay focused on one thing at a time.

I hope you'll seriously consider your own stacking order. If you do, you'll discover a pace that's just right for your own temperament. This will make the creation of abundance a much richer experience in every sense of the word.

42.

DON'T PANIC!

Just as Chicken Little was dead wrong when she said the sky was falling, it's important to keep your perspective even when it feels like she was right. Remember, when something is falling, it rarely keeps falling. There cycles in life.

An excellent example of where huge profits have been realized has been the California real estate market. In my lifetime, the cycle has gone way up and way down many times. Yet the one consistency in the fluctuations has been the tendency for many people to freak out and panic when times are bad, to assume the downturn is going to last forever, that things can only get worse. In retrospect, we can see that, often, the best time to get in is when everyone else is panicking.

In business, people panic about practically everything—missed deadlines, orders not received, comments by others, fear of mistakes, negative trends. You name it and someone has panicked about it. Yet I've never seen even a single instance where the panic actually helped to solve the problem. Instead, panic is neutral at best and greatly interferes at worst. Panic tends to bring out the worst in everyone. It makes others (and you) feel tense and fearful. It increases the likelihood of mistakes, missed opportunities, and miscommunication.

Nothing interferes with the creation of success and abundance like panic. When you make the commitment to stop panicking, you'll notice some incredible things happening. First, you'll notice that a vast majority of what you are most worried about will never happen, or it won't be as bad as you first thought. It was Benjamin Franklin who said, "Some terrible things happened in my lifetime—a few of which actually happened." By avoiding the panic, you won't waste time, anxiety, and energy trying to solve what probably doesn't need solving. Second, when you learn to keep your bearings, your wisdom will come forth. In the absence of worry, answers will emerge. Instead of a head full of concerns, you'll create a head full of solutions. Finally, when you stay calm, you really do bring out the best in others. Many people react to the feelings of others. If you can maintain your bearings, chances are the people you work with will, too.

Life is far too short to worry it away. To bring forth your greatest potential, eliminate panic altogether from your thinking. This will put you on a path toward abundance.

43.

CREATE FROM THE INSIDE OUT

You can work long and hard, be creative, clever, talented, insightful, even lucky—but if you fail to understand the importance of your own thoughts in the process of creation, it will all be for naught.

The single most important factor of success, abundance, and the creation of prosperity comes from within yourself—your thoughts. As James Allen reminds us in *As a Man Thinketh*, "A particular train of thought persisted in, be it good or bad, cannot fail to produce its results on the character and circumstances. A man cannot directly choose his circumstances, but he can choose his thoughts, and so indirectly, yet surely, shape his circumstances."

If you could look into the minds of successful men and women you would discover a wealth of positive energy—thoughts of success and abundance, and a complete lack of doubt. In order to create external prosperity, you must first create *thoughts* of prosperity. You must see yourself as successful, play out your dreams and ambitions in your mind—successfully.

It's tempting to convince yourself that you would become more positive and that your thoughts would become purer and more success-oriented *after* a measure of success. However, this is clearly putting the cart before the horse. The quickest, surest way to riches is from the inside out. Thoughts have tremendous power. Use your imagination to create your dreams, and great changes will quickly follow suit. Once again, James Allen: "Let a man radically alter his thoughts, and he will be astonished at the rapid transformation it will effect in the material conditions of his life."

I've known many successful people in many different fields. Although they have vastly different talents, temperaments, skills, work ethics, and backgrounds, they all have one thing in common. This golden thread of consistency is that each of them sees him or herself as successful. They never question this fact; they can't understand why anyone would question their own level of greatness. It's hard for them to understand why everyone isn't successful because, to them, the formula is quite simple: Success originates in the mind and translates into the material world. It doesn't work the other way around, as so many seem to believe. Successful people know that the one aspect of life that they do have control over is their own thinking. All of us have this same advantage, so let's all start there!

44.

BANISH YOUR DOUBT

In your dreams you are able to do some remarkable things— be two places at once, shift scenes and environments, walk through walls, become rich and famous, overcome great obstacles, get along with your parents, become the CEO, create great abundance, write a bestseller, speak to a million people, to name just a few. And through it all, you never, ever doubt your abilities. In fact, can you imagine how ridiculous it would be to question your abilities while dreaming? Can you imagine saying, "Wait a minute, I can't do that?" And in your dreams, how often do you fail? Rarely. But if you do, it's always for a specific purpose—to learn something, to test your strength, to overcome great odds, to take you to the next level of growth. Because you don't doubt yourself, all things are possible.

Yet in our waking state, most of us spend a great deal of energy every day of our lives, doubting our abilities—to our great detriment. We doubt ourselves at practically every turn; we doubt our abilities to write well, speak to a group, come up with a new idea or solution, overcome an obstacle, create a better mousetrap, market a product or service, or negotiate with a difficult person. We question our self-worth, how much we deserve to be paid, or how valuable or talented we are to an organization or as an entrepreneur. We doubt our ability to overcome rejection, start over, or confront a challenge.

A surefire strategy for success is to banish doubt from your life—all of it. This doesn't mean you should start doing foolish things or making childish decisions. It means you should start trusting in yourself, creating an inner knowing, an awareness that you have everything it takes to be an absolute winner, to make your dreams come true. The only true obstacle lies within the doubt itself—and all doubt lies within your own thoughts.

For years I convinced myself that I couldn't speak in front of groups. I believed this self-imposed limitation with all my heart. I even had concrete evidence that my belief was true; as I mentioned earlier, twice I fainted while trying to speak. Then one day a friend and mentor put me on the spot in front of a large group. Before it was my turn to speak, he turned to me and said, "Richard, the idea that you aren't capable of speaking to a group is absolutely preposterous. Dismiss this crazy notion from your mind and everything will be fine. Get over it, now!" I remember his words as if they were said this morning. He was right. Speaking became effortless the *moment* I banished the doubt from my mind.

You can do the same thing. It's silly to hold on to any doubt in your life. It does no good. All doubt is a waste of energy and interferes with your natural ability to create the abundance and wealth that is your birthright. Whatever doubts are lingering in your mind, let them go. It's far easier than you think, and will produce great rewards.

45.

KNOW THE SECRET OF SILENCE

There is a tendency in business (and in life) to want to actively engage ourselves in the process of creation. We want to know the answers. We want to figure out what to do next. We want to think our way to success. However, in many instances—I believe in most instances—the best answers come not from programmed, memory-based thinking but from the silence within. In fact, I've watched many people (and I've done it, too) think their way out of success by overanalyzing a situation.

Have you ever noticed that when you are quiet and still, calm and silent, you know exactly what to do? Being silent doesn't shut down your mind, it only activates a deeper type of intelligence. No one knows for sure where this deeper intelligence comes from, or what it's called, but all wise cultures are certain that it exists. When we are silent, it's as if we tap into a universal source of wisdom. It's as though our thinking comes to us rather than us having to actively pursue our thoughts. It's as if we get the benefit of "universal thought" instead of having to rely on our own limited thinking.

Learning to trust in silence is simple because, when you do, the results are so spectacular. Once you get the hang of it your life will become far easier and less stressful. Success will sneak up on you. The next time you need an answer that is not readily available, rather than racking your brain over it, try an experiment. Instead of actively thinking about the issue, let it go. The fact that you know the nature of the problem or question is all the information you need. Allow the question to settle, like silt in water. When you do this, something magical begins to happen within your consciousness. Something beyond you, a dimension of thought over which you have no control, flips on. And like the back burner of a stove, the question or problem begins to bubble. In time—it may be a few minutes, hours, or days depending on the issue—an answer will pop into your head. There will be no struggle and no effort. It will just happen. You may be surprised, but you'll certainly be delighted at the wisdom that comes through. Be careful, however, to not take yourself too seriously. The wisdom you experience comes not from you but from the silence. I guess I'm letting the secret out of the bag!

46.

SOCK AWAY TWO YEARS OF LIVING EXPENSES

On the surface, it might seem that the suggestion to scrimp and save, to put money aside for an entire year or two, could be contrary to the message of this book—to not worry. After all, isn't saving for a rainy day based on worry and fear? It all depends on how you look at it.

Several years ago I heard a super-successful financial guru explain that the single most important thing he *ever* did for himself, prior to becoming rich, was to set aside two years of living expenses. Although it required enormous sacrifice, discipline, hard work, and patience—and although it took a full five years to save this much money—it paid enormous dividends, especially psychologically. Essentially, what it did was to give him enormous peace of mind, the freedom he needed to take risks that would be difficult, if not impossible, without this financial cushion. Very simply, socking away a few years of living expenses allowed him to avoid worry, to pursue dreams and interesting opportunities.

I heard a story of a man who was offered a job at a promising and exciting start-up computer company back in the early seventies. Because he had implemented a strategy of having plenty of financial reserve, he was able to accept the job—without fear—which included a relatively small initial salary but a ton of stock, and stock options, in the company. He had no worries whatsoever. If the venture worked out, terrific. If it didn't, it was at least a valuable experience. The man, however, was not the first person chosen for this job. Someone else was the first choice. This man had virtually no savings. He was extremely bright and talented, and making an excellent salary. But, like so many people, he was living paycheck to paycheck. He had a big mortgage and both he and his wife drove very expensive cars, they enjoyed fine restaurants, and their four children attended private schools. They spent most of what they made. Although the job offer sounded like the best opportunity of his lifetime, he decided to decline—too risky! He was too worried. Looking back, he says, "If I'd had enough discipline to save in my early years, it would have been a no-brainer. I would most certainly have taken the job."

To make a long story short: The man who took the risk amassed a huge fortune in less than a decade. His psychological ability to take the risk turned him into a multimillionaire. The other man, who also wanted the job but was too worried, still lives paycheck to paycheck well into his sixties. His abundance was severely limited by his sense of worry.

The moral of the story is obvious. Unless you are extremely lucky, creating abundance usually involves at least some risk taking. However, if you are absolutely, completely dependent on a secure, regular salary, if you are fearful that you are a paycheck away from homelessness, you are probably going to dismiss many opportunities that come your way.

It's well worth the tradeoff—fewer vacations; a less expensive car, home, and clothing; fewer evenings out on the town; as well as many other luxuries, even necessities—for that two years of income in the bank. It's amazing how more creative you can be—appropriately aggressive, and willing to experiment with new and/or unusual opportunities—when your very livelihood isn't dependent on your day-to-day efforts. So, starting today, begin your "rainy day" fund. A few years from now you'll be able to spend it—or give it away. In fact, you'll be able to do just about anything you want to do.

47.

GIVE UP YOUR FEAR OF DISAPPROVAL

How many people choose careers and career directions based on what other people—parents, relatives, professors, friends—think they should do. "You should be a doctor, lawyer, pilot, musician" can be a very powerful message, especially when it's repeated often and associated with status, prestige, social approval, and other psychological accolades.

Here's one simple example of someone I know: Stephen was informed at a very young age that he was going to make his parents proud by becoming a lawyer. He grew up knowing that this was the only way to please Mom and Dad. All the relatives expected this would be his chosen path. The family spoke of the "up-and-coming lawyer" often throughout the years. Two members of the family were lawyers. Both had become very successful, and everyone in the family looked up to them.

In time, Stephen did, in fact, become a lawyer. The problem was, he not only detested the field of law but was also frustrated by his surprising difficulty in making any significant money. Aspects of law that some of his friends and colleagues found intriguing and exciting he found boring and difficult. He struggled for years before he thought he was going to go crazy.

Through a short stint of gentle counseling, Stephen discovered that his fear of disappointing his parents had forced him into a career that gave him no satisfaction whatsoever. His counselor convinced him that the fear of disapproval can interfere with our greatest chance of success.

After his counseling sessions enlightened him as to the source of this fear, he visited a career counselor and discovered through a series of tests that his aptitude for law was among the lowest 4 percent of all lawyers that had been tested. No wonder he was failing in his career! He was barely qualified. The tests showed that he was far more suited to such fields as marketing and promotion. He decided to take a chance and change directions. He not only loved his new field, but he flourished as well. Many of his marketing ideas were real winners and he quickly became a "hot commodity." His financial life quickly turned around to the point where, today, he is quite wealthy and, more important, very happy.

The message of this strategy is enormously important: Our best chance of success is obtained through the elimination of fear. This includes the fear of disapproval from others. Examine the reasons why you entered your chosen field. Was it out of joy and genuine interest? This is where abundance can be found. Or was there an element of pleasing Mom and Dad, or someone else? Did you do it for the attention you thought you were going to get? If the answer to these questions is "yes," it might be time to investigate something new. If necessary, talk to a psychologist or a career counselor who might be able to shed some light on the subject, or offer some helpful guidance. Whatever it takes, it's well worth the effort. If you change direction and do something because you truly love it, instead of because you think it's the "right thing to do," your path toward success might be closer than you ever dreamed possible.

48.

KEEP A LIST OF BARGAIN SHOPPING PLACES
IN YOUR PURSE OR WALLET

I'm the last person I would have ever expected to implement, much less write about, this strategy. However, the savings potential is so huge, it would almost be a crime not to mention it. This idea is really simple; all it takes to get started is a pencil and a small pad of paper.

Everybody seems to have the same problem when they go out to shop for consumer goods or to a restaurant. You are positive that in the past year or so, you have seen or heard about a great restaurant that you want to try, or a factory store that seemed just right for your next Christmas or birthday shopping trip, or some other place that offered a great deal on something you might be interested in acquiring. Months go by, and virtually no one is able to remember that special, bargain place. This seems to be particularly true in large metropolitan areas. Since you can't remember and don't have easy access to the places you've heard about, you end up spending far more than you would have otherwise had to.

The solution is simple and extremely practical. Simply keep an organized, updated list of places you hear about in your purse or wallet. You may hear of these places from friends or neighbors, or by listening to the radio. You can also save thousands of dollars each year if you call your reference librarian to locate the best shoppers' guide. The reference librarian's salary is paid out of your tax dollars and she is there to help you. The shoppers' guide represents thousands of hours of research. The authors of these guides dedicate a good portion of their lives to searching out the best values in your area, and it's yours for the asking. The bargains that you find result from limited selection, sometimes missing sizes, and close-out items that cannot be returned, bulk buying, discontinued merchandise, stores going out of business for one reason or another, as well as a variety of other factors.

A friend of mine recently shared with me a success story that came about because of this idea. For about a year he had been keeping a list of bargain stores that he had heard about. His wedding anniversary was coming up and he decided to get a special gift for his wife. She had really been wanting a new bracelet. So he took a quick look over his list and noticed that he had jotted down the name of a large jeweler that was going out of business. He made a call and discovered that the store would be closing for good in less than a week. He made the thirty-minute drive and found an absolutely beautiful bracelet at a fraction of the original cost. His savings: 75 percent! Had he not had this "bargain list" at his disposal, he would have spent far more than was really necessary.

This strategy also comes in handy if you find yourself buying lots of birthday presents for children or wedding gifts for newlyweds. It really pays off and I highly recommend you give it a try.

49.

DON'T RELY ON TOO MUCH DATA

It's often the case that when people get worried or frightened, they focus too much on data in an effort to alleviate their anxiety—to make themselves feel better. The assumption is, "If I can figure everything out, everything will be okay." So worried stockbrokers will stare at their computer screens, gathering data instead of making calls and selling stock. Managers in organizations will study reports and financials but will avoid taking actions that will make things work smoother and smarter. And salespeople who are afraid to go out and make sales calls, or who are fearful of rejection in one way or another, will spend countless hours reading sales literature or sending out direct-mail pieces, but they won't go out and take risks, make the calls, or ask for the sale. All this "data gathering" may satisfy their curiosity and buy some time, but it will do little in a positive sense to affect the bottom line.

Of course, it's simple to justify our actions, decisions, and the way we actually spend our time, especially when we're frightened. We can always rationalize that what were doing is necessary and important—the more information we have at our disposal, the better. Right? Sometimes this is true, but not always.

There's a point where excessive information can interfere with going out and actually making money. Too much data can convince us that we're too busy to do what it takes to really succeed; it can convince us that our actions are too risky, too premature. And, of course, sometimes we'll be right. However, this is the exception rather than the rule. More often than not, too much data can fill our heads with worrisome, fearful thoughts that keep us between where we are and where we want to be. A favorite quote of mine suggests that "If we had to overcome every possible objection before we got started, then nothing—absolutely nothing—would ever get accomplished." I have found that excessive data gathering, too much mulling over the same set of facts, is very often the major factor that encourages us to overcome every possible objection before *we* get started, before *we* go out and do what it takes.

The next time you find yourself filling your head with facts and stewing over data, take a step back. See if what you're doing is really going to help you out, make things better—or are you simply postponing the steps that will actually bring about abundance? Be completely honest with yourself. Perhaps, instead of studying facts, you should pick up the phone and make a call. It's very possible you have all the data you need and the simple decision to stop worrying is the most important thing you could be doing.

50.

FIND A MENTOR

It's simple, common sense that if someone wanted to be a journeyman plumber, he or she would be wise to find someone who either has retired or is about to retire from the plumbing field to act as a source of guidance, advice, and inspiration. It's helpful to have someone you can share an occasional cup of coffee with, kick around ideas—someone you can to turn to, ask questions of, seek guidance from, philosophize.

I've never seen or even heard of someone moving backward as a result of finding a mentor. Yet when I ask around, very few people, as an overall percentage, admit to having one.

I have had several mentors in my life who have helped me enormously in many aspects of life—business, money making, investments, marketing, public speaking, even physical fitness. Both the mentor and the student get a great deal out of the relationship, it's an ideal tradeoff. The advantages to the student are obvious: confidence, camaraderie, ideas—a road map to follow. For the mentor, there's the joy of helping, feeling appreciated and needed, the fun of teaching, the privilege of reviewing what he or she did right over the years, the idea of passing the torch. It's a blessing to know that your ideas are being used by someone else.

Often you can find a mentor through your own networking circle—an older friend, someone with whom you have built a relationship over the years, someone you respect and enjoy spending time with. Typically, a mentor is someone who enjoys sharing his or her ideas. It isn't necessary that you formalize your relationship by calling this person a "mentor," only that you have a mutual understanding that you are willing to sit down together or at least talk on the phone, on a somewhat regular basis—once a month, once every other month, whatever. Make it clear that your intention is to learn all you can. These days, it's easier than ever to find a mentor. While nothing takes the place of personal contacts—networking with people who love you and/or care about your success—there are, if need be, mentoring agencies that will help match mentors with students. Don't let anything stand in the way of finding an excellent, caring mentor. You will avoid many unnecessary mistakes and reap the rewards for years to come. Often, the best way to pay back your mentor is to promise him or her that, once you are in a position to do so, you'll do the same for someone else.

51.

DELIGHT IN THE SUCCESS OF OTHERS

Let's be honest here. Have you ever found yourself secretly wishing someone else would fail? I don't mean you wish them any serious bad luck, only that they don't become even more successful than you? Sometimes it's hard to wish others well, particularly those you know well—friends, colleagues, neighbors, family members. It's hard to see a colleague get the promotion you worked so hard for. It's difficult to see your kid sister on television, or your neighbor able to purchase a new car. We're human; we get jealous. I've had clients who were even a little jealous of their own spouse's success.

While it can be seductive, or at least habitual, to secretly desire to keep others at your level, it's absolutely, positively not in your best interest. The way to rise to the top is to wish everyone well, to hope with all your heart that everyone can expand to their greatest potential, to wish that the people you know, and those whom you don't know, can all realize their dreams and achieve greatness.

It's critical to know that there is plenty of success to go around. In fact, as people achieve their goals, the pie gets even bigger for the rest of us. We don't want to see one another at our lowest common denominator, but at our highest common vision. We can *all* succeed and each time someone does—anyone—it helps the rest of us.

When you wish someone well, it creates a momentum within you, an inner environment of success. It reminds your spirit of your loving and deserving nature. It creates the atmosphere within you to help you succeed and create abundance. When you delight in the success of others, it's as if you are sprinkling the seeds for a garden of success.

As you wish others well, notice how good it feels. When your wishes are sincere, they will serve as a reminder that giving and receiving are two sides of the same coin. Truly, it feels as good to see someone else succeed as it does to succeed yourself. Start delighting in the success of others and watch your own level of greatness soar!

52.

ASK YOURSELF,

WHERE IS THIS DECISION LIKELY TO LEAD?

Many of us follow certain paths simply because they present themselves. Often, however, these paths lead you in directions or take you to places you really don't want to be. You can save yourself enormous amounts of time and energy by asking the simple, straightforward question, Where is this decision likely to lead? And then, pay close attention to your answer.

There is a story about "the trip to Abilene," and it goes something like this: There were four friends sitting on a porch in a small town in Texas. It was a really hot day, well over a hundred degrees. Someone mentioned that there was a good restaurant over in Abilene, some two hundred miles away. The road wasn't paved and the car had no air-conditioning. Without knowing why, the four friends somehow ended up in the boiling hot car, headed toward Abilene. It was miserable. The ride was bumpy and extremely hot. All four friends were frustrated and angry.

When they finally arrived in Abilene some five hours later, one of the friends, in a frustrated tone, asked, "Why are we here anyway?" One of the others replied, rather confidently, "I thought *you* wanted to come." "I didn't want to come here, I thought you did," was the response.

To make a potentially long story short, no one had the slightest interest in being in Abilene. Each person thought someone else really wanted to be there. No one thought to ask, Where is this decision likely to lead? No one asked, Why are we really going?

How many family get-togethers or business meetings are like this?

Aren't there times when no one *really* wants to be there but everyone came because each assumed that everyone else wanted to?

Sometimes in business we take our own "trips to Abilene." For example, sometimes therapists or consultants, when opening a private practice, will decide to work on weekends and charge half of what everyone else charges. This way, they believe, they will build up their practice faster and easier. This assumption is far from true. If you ask the question, Where is this decision likely to lead?, you'll get some pretty scary, yet predictable answers. In this instance, you'll begin to fill up your business with people who can only see you on weekends. Your clients will get used to it, and most of your referrals will be people who expect to see you on weekends—probably during the time your spouse is *off* work or the time of your favorite football game. You'll be stuck! As far as the reduced fee goes, again, you're setting yourself up to fail. If you undercharge for your service, your clients will tell all their friends how wonderful and fair you are because you are so incredibly inexpensive! Pretty soon you'll have a full practice—and you'll be going broke! I had a client who couldn't resist the temptation to take on new territory for the product he was selling. What he didn't consider, however, was that if he succeeded (which he did), the quality of his life would suffer (which it did). As he made his decision to expand, he ignored the fact that he would be spending an *additional* twenty hours a week driving in his car. In retrospect, he believes that he would have been far better off focusing on his existing territory and building his business within a reasonable geographic area. Again, the issue would have been easily avoided had he asked himself the million-dollar question.

It's always a good idea to ask yourself, Where is this decision likely to lead? When you do, you can avoid many hassles and mistakes that are otherwise inevitable. By asking this simple question, you can keep your energy directed in areas that will serve you and others well.

53.

REMEMBER THE GOLDEN RULE

Do you remember the golden rule that most of us were taught as youngsters? It goes like this: Do unto others as you would have them do unto you. What are some other ways of saying this magical formula? Let's see. What goes around, comes around. As you treat others, so shall you be treated. If you don't have something nice to say, don't say anything at all. There are many variations of this, and it's one of the first lessons we try to teach our children.

This must be one of the simplest, most easily implementable formulas for the creation of abundance. Simply put, all you have to do to ensure that you will be treated fairly, respectfully, and with kindness—and to ensure that others will reach out to help you and praise you—is to do these things yourself!

Become a thoughtful person. Offer assistance. Be nice. Reach out to others. Become even more generous. Say "Thank you." These, and hundreds of other similar little gestures, are the ways you can reach out and tell the world you care.

Giving and receiving *are* two sides of the same coin. They are different manifestations of the same universal energy. Ultimately, what you offer to the world is exactly what you get back. So, if your goal is to create a joyful life filled with abundance, the most important thing you can do is help others do the same. This is one area of life you can control. You can control how generous you are. You do have the capacity to offer praise and help, to be of service, and to be kind to others.

Don't make the mistake of becoming upset or frustrated if your acts of kindness don't come back immediately. The universe has its own set of rules and its own sense of timing. Be patient and loving. If you are committed to the Golden Rule, it's only a matter of time before your life will be filled with everything you desire.

54

DON'T BE FRIGHTENED TO ASK FOR REFERRALS

In virtually any type of business that you're trying to expand, referrals are the key. Whether you're trying to build a private practice, grow a business, even build up your nonprofit fund-raising efforts, it's essential to ask for help. It's critical to get others involved, to get people talking about you in a positive way, spreading the word.

Many business experts agree that the single greatest source of failure can be traced to the *fear* of asking for referrals—asking for business, asking for help, or asking for the sale. I would agree. Generally speaking, people *are* frightened to ask for help. They would rather stay small but safe than take a risk and grow. The truth, however, as we know, is that staying frightened is not safe at all. Ultimately, fear will be the downfall of most businesses. Again, to make money, it's critical that you don't worry.

Here's a simple example of how simply asking for referrals would be of tremendous help. My family and I are regular patrons of a local restaurant. We are probably among its most consistent and loyal customers. We praise the owner and the chef on a regular basis. We let them know how much we appreciate their skill and hard work. And we keep coming back. While the food is fantastic and the people are wonderful, the restaurant isn't doing as well as it could be. Its location is questionable in terms of visibility, and they engage in absolutely no marketing.

Here's the interesting part. While we have proven that we are on their side, while we have demonstrated again and again that we want them to succeed, the owner has never, ever asked for our help. He has never asked us to bring in other friends, pass out menus, or even tell others about his fine restaurant.

Can you imagine what would happen to his business if he would simply ask us, and his other loyal customers—people he knows quite well—to help him? My guess is that he would have a waiting list every night of the week; people would be crowding outside the door for a chance to get in! He could, for example, say to me: "Richard, I know you really love this restaurant. The next few times you come in, would you consider bringing in some friends so that more people can try us out? If you do, I'll only charge you half price (or he could offer a bottle of wine on the house, or a free meal, or a coupon for a reduced-price meal next time, or something else altogether).

There are many people (I'm one of them) who delight in the success of others, and would therefore almost be embarrassed not to be of help once asked. You might be thinking, "If you really wanted to bring friends into the restaurant, wouldn't you do so anyway?" Not necessarily. People go to restaurants for different reasons. One of ours is simply to relax, to be spontaneous. When I'm thinking about a restaurant, I'm usually thinking about my own needs and preferences and those of my family. However, I also love to be of service to someone else if I'm asked, especially if I really like the person.

It doesn't take much effort for me to call a friend or two and ask them to join us. I've probably been looking for an excuse to get together with them anyway. Here's the perfect opportunity. I get to see a good friend *and* help out the owner of the restaurant. By simply using referrals as a source of new business, this owner (and millions like him) could double, even triple his existing clientele in a very short period of time.

This principle applies to virtually any kind of business you are attempting to expand. Not all, but most people really want to help. Go ahead and ask. You'll be amazed at how quickly your business will grow! (P.S. I'm going to give the restaurant owner a copy of this book!)

55.

KNOW THAT THE IDEA "OPPORTUNITY ONLY KNOCKS ONCE" IS A BIG MYTH

It's hard to imagine a belief that is based more on fear than this one. Yet this idea is so common to our collective consciousness that it has turned into a cliché. People actually believe they are being wise by accepting this silly limitation. Yet when they do, it's as if they're saying to themselves and to the world, "My creative days are over. I'm a complete package. My life has been lived out." Nonsense!

When someone says "Opportunity only knocks once," what in the world are they thinking? Opportunity exists virtually everywhere you look. There are thousands of new business opportunities being created as we speak. There are millions more that need to be improved upon, thus an unlimited supply of additional opportunities. There are wonderful jobs being created each day—new partnerships being formed, new projects being started, new products and technologies being invented. There are books that need to be written, children that need to be taught, houses that need to be cleaned and others that need to be built. There are people, in fact entire cultures, who need help—so many people can benefit from and need our unique creativity. We all have gifts and talents to offer. We live in a world of unlimited potential, a world of creative genius. All that is required to succeed is to know, not just hope, that there is plenty to go around.

If you buy into the belief that opportunity only knocks once, you may jump on board too quickly when something that looks like an opportunity presents itself. You may take a job that you don't really like, or move to a location that doesn't suit your temperament. Instead of picking and choosing wisely, from a place of wisdom, joy, and common sense, you may end up reacting impulsively. On the other hand, because fear clouds your vision, you may miss out on wonderful opportunities when they come your way. Your fear may convince you to wait for something else because this one is too risky, or too scary, or beyond you, or whatever. Fear squeezes out opportunity from both ends.

When you let go of the fear that there isn't enough to go around, opportunities will fall into your lap. The absence of fear will clarify your goals and help you see beyond the risks. Knowing that opportunity *isn't* a once-in-a-lifetime event gives you the confidence to explore your options and to keep your mind open to new opportunities. Your eyes will see new ways of doing things; they will see opportunities, even in past failures. You'll realize that your chances have been there all along; you simply haven't seen them.

Let go of your fear. The universe has an infinite supply of opportunity. There is plenty to go around. You may be surprised to see that something is coming your way right now.

56

LOOK FOR EXPENDITURES THAT MIGHT BE MADE
COOPERATIVELY INSTEAD OF INDIVIDUALLY

A client of mine shared with me the very clever way that he financed his new business. He lived on a private road with only seven houses. He loved his home, but taking care of it had become quite a financial burden. Living in the country, it seemed that there was always something else to purchase—a lawn mower, a ladder, a used pickup truck, or a chain saw. Of course, everything he bought also had to be maintained, insured, and serviced. Although he couldn't afford it, he also felt he could really use a tractor. How was he ever going to afford to start that business?

Then, inspiration struck. Hmmm! He wondered if his neighbors felt the same way he did about the cost of living in the country. As it turned out, they did. To make a long story short, they had a community meeting and decided that, whenever possible, they would purchase one item for the entire street instead of seven that would be sitting in their garages a majority of the time. They developed a formula that included selling many of their existing things and using the money to repurchase collective items. They would share one pickup truck instead of seven, one chain saw, and one branch shredder.

Obviously, not everything could be bought collectively or agreed upon, and there were plenty of details and a few hassles to work out regarding storage, maintenance, scheduling, decision making, ownership, and liability. But so what? The almost unbelievable savings were well worth it. In their case, the street ended up with a truck, a tractor, and virtually everything else one would need to run an effective and efficient farm. They found it was infinitely easier to maintain one item collectively than it was seven items all by themselves. Over time, the cost per family was reduced to around 25 percent of what it had been. This simple idea ended up saving each family thousands of dollars per year. My client was easily able to open his business without financial worry. Another family on the street was able to start a college fund, and yet another was able to take a trip to Hawaii. But this was just the beginning of the benefits. The financial benefits of this type of "cooperative purchasing" last for years and years because each year you avoid *wasting* your money, it gives you more operating capital to create the abundance you desire. The environment also benefits by having far less waste and drain of resources.

Needless to say, most people don't live on a seven-home private drive. But the general concept is the same regardless of where you live. Whenever possible, try to purchase items collectively instead of individually. Often, the most thought about items in a discussion such as this one are big-ticket items—a second home, a boat, or membership in a club. Yet smaller, less expensive items can also be considered. If you are the same size as a sister or a friend, why not consider combining some of your clothing expenses? How often do you wear that $100 sweater anyway? Many people save over $1,000 per year simply by buying a few things together! Are you thinking of going out and buying camping gear? Realistically, how often are you going to use it? Once a year if you're lucky. The rest of the time it will sit in the garage or the attic, along with your skis, bicycles, and other sporting gear. Wouldn't it be wise to gather a few friends together and share this expense? This way you can get the best possible equipment at a tiny fraction of the cost. And you'll never, ever know the difference.

Or you can combine a shopping trip and make your purchases in larger quantity, usually resulting in significant savings. For people who live within city limits, it pays to have one automobile shared among two or even three friends. I have two friends who really wanted to join a wine club. The problem was, neither of them drank enough wine to warrant joining. A perfect solution was for them to join together. Even really small purchases can be made jointly. Do any of your friends subscribe to the same magazines as you do? What about the newspaper? What do you do with these things after you read them? Wouldn't it be easy to share some of these things and combine the expenses with neighbors and/or friends? Chances are, if you look carefully at what your needs actually are, you can save a small fortune by combining a few of your purchases with others. This will free up some needed capital, greatly reduce your waste, as well as your financial worry. Plus, owning something with someone else can be a lot of fun. Try it, I'll bet you'll like it!

57.

SHOP CAREFULLY WITH
YOUR VACATION DOLLARS

Although this isn't really a book on clever ways to save money, I couldn't resist this one. Sometimes, saving money, especially a great deal of money, is one of the easiest ways to keep your net worth moving in the right direction. One of the greatest ways to ensure a worry-free vacation is to know that you are getting not only all the fun but also the best possible vacation value. That way you can relax and not worry about the cost.

Many people know that one of the easiest ways to spend a big chunk of their potential retirement savings is to call a name hotel in some exotic spot such as Honolulu. You can save about two-thirds of that expense, however, if you are willing to spend the tiny amount of effort it takes to rent a vacation condominium, possibly only a few blocks away from the other facility. You can, of course, pay top rent for that condo by dealing with a local agency, or save approximately half or more by taking a one-month subscription to the Honolulu newspaper. That puts you in touch with individuals who want to rent their own condominium or home.

If you are in a position to own a second home and feel you must have one, consider this idea. A friend of mine wanted to own a condominium in Maui. He knew that, statistically, virtually everyone who owns a vacation home reports that the two happiest days in owning them are the day they bought it and the day they sold it. The simple truth is, vacation homes are rarely used and tie up money that could be put to work elsewhere.

Still, this friend couldn't resist, so here's what he did. He knew that he would spend between two and four weeks a year there, at most. So he formed a cooperative group of ten owners plus himself. Each of the ten owners purchased one-tenth of the condominium and obtained the use of it for one month, each year. For taking the risk, and for his work and effort in putting the group together, he obtained two months of usage. Each tenancy-in-common owner can either use the property for that month, assign it to friends, or rent it to strangers. This is called a private time share and costs each owner about one-third or one-fourth of what they would pay in a public time share. In addition, each owner gets to use the property for a full month instead of the ordinary one to two weeks. In this instance, the property has more than doubled in value, and my friend and his associates are happy campers. Shopping wisely with your vacation dollars virtually ensures that you will spend less of your precious time worrying about the costs.

58.

DECIDE CAREFULLY BETWEEN A FIXED
AND VARIABLE INTEREST RATE
ON YOUR HOME MORTGAGE

This particular financial decision is a classic example of one that is virtually always made with a sense of worry. But worrying about this decision has the potential to cost you tens of thousands of unnecessary dollars. Just think what could happen if all that money was working for you instead of against you.

From time to time, there is a considerable difference between the cost of a variable-rate home mortgage and the cost of a fixed-rate mortgage. It is certainly okay to pay a little money to reduce anxiety, but it's not at all necessary to pay too much.

Obviously, no one has the benefit of a crystal ball. If you select a fixed rate and inflation and interest rates stay low in the future, you will certainly regret it. However, if you select a variable rate and we have renewed inflation and high interest rates, you will also regret it.

Many people assume, out of pure and simple fear, however, that high inflation and high interest rates will be back—they are inevitable. Thus, worriers believe, going with a fixed-rate mortgage is always a wise thing to do. But is that fear realistic, or is it simply misguided worry?

Although this subject is probably best discussed in a textbook on economics, I believe it's also a fascinating example of how worry can interfere with the creation of abundance. Instead of relaxing and appreciating the fact that, as a country, we have learned from our past mistakes, thus taking advantage of extremely low variable rates, many of us remain in an unrealistic state of fear. We believe that we are "being safe."

Here are a few facts. Before 1979, the U.S. Federal Reserve Bank pursued a policy of "targeting interest rates" instead of targeting money supply growth. Most economists believe that inflation is a result of a money supply that outgrows the production of the economy. In simple terms, you have too much money chasing too few products. This is what happened in the decade of the seventies. The Federal Reserve had a kind of arrogance that allowed them to believe that they could target the appropriate interest rate to keep inflation in check. What a disaster! Since then, however, the Federal Reserve, operating a little like a reformed drunk, has pursued a stable money growth policy. And because of this major change, many economists believe that hyperinflation is a thing of the past, and that fears should be buried for good. Who knows for sure? But this is what the experts believe.

Mortgage broker friends have told me that the typical homeowner who selects a fixed-rate loan says something like, "I'm worried. I can't take the chance; interest rates may go up and I'll lose money." It's actually a wiser and more accurate statement to say that the homeowner takes a chance of gain or loss *regardless* of his or her decision. If a person derives all of his income from a fixed-payment pension plan, it might make sense for him to select a fixed-rate mortgage payment. However, the overwhelming majority of homeowners do not have fixed incomes. If inflation should return, most homeowners will receive an adjustment of wages, social security, profits, company bonuses, and interest on savings.

Most economists now believe that depressions are essentially obsolete because, as a society, we know more about how business cycles work, and we certainly know better what not to do. Since the Great Depression we have had several recessions, and some have been more painful than others.

However, nothing has even approached the severity of the Great Depression, and probably only a classic doomsayer still believes that there is any possibility of a recurrence of such an event.

Thus, I believe that the decision to select a fixed-rate loan over a variable-rate loan is based mainly on worry, and may turn out to be the incorrect decision most of the time. Although there are no guarantees, if one makes a decision based on actual information instead of on fear, he or she will probably make a wiser decision.

59.

BUY LARGE DEDUCTIBLE INSURANCE

Very few people would question the value of certain types of insurance. The level of your chosen deductible, however, is essential in a clear-headed financial plan. Generally speaking, you should always select the highest possible deductible that your insurer allows—and invest the difference in yourself. The less you worry, the more you save!

From a certain perspective (and be assured I'm not arguing against insurance), *all* insurance is based on fear. You have an asset—your car, home, business, earning capacity, even your health—and you are afraid that, at some point, something is going to happen to that asset: you will die or get sick, your car will be stolen or damaged, or your home or business will burn to the ground. Insurance is provided to protect you against these and other fears. Of course, some worries are more likely to occur than others. For example, while everyone eventually dies, not everyone will get into a car accident. Or most people will probably need medical attention at some point, but only a tiny percentage will ever be sued. Your job, as a consumer, is to carefully select which worries you most want to protect yourself against.

Since a vast majority of the things you fear the most will never actually happen, it works to your advantage to select the highest possible deductible on all insurance plans—therefore paying the lowest possible premiums. Then, be absolutely sure to invest the difference.

Just the other day I was listening to a radio talk show. The guest was a retired expert on "consumer product insurance." He was discussing the pros and cons of "extended warranties" on vehicles, electronics, and other products. His conclusion was that there were no real "pros" and that, to some degree, the entire industry was a "con." He said that less than 25 percent of the premiums paid were ever actually used. His conclusion was that, statistically, the consumer was far better off sticking the extended warranty premium into a rainy day account where it is likely never to be used. If, for some unlikely reason, you do suffer a loss, you'll still have the money available to make the necessary repairs. If not, you can use the money as a down payment the next time you purchase the item in question.

The math on this type of decision is fairly obvious. Why, then, do most people select a very low deductible and pay outrageous prices on their insurance? Fear is the answer.

When you distinguish between reasonable financial concerns and decisions based solely on fear, you can free up a great deal of financial as well as emotional power. The trick is to be courageous enough to admit that your fear is not working to your advantage and to be truthful about where your decision is coming from. Remember, fear keeps you focused on little details and unlikely events. It's far wiser to assume the best—know that most of the time your fears will not manifest.

60.

WHISTLE WHILE YOU WORK

It's amazing what happens when you act as if you love what you do. The positive energy helps not only you but everyone around you. It's contagious. A positive attitude brings forth creativity and aliveness in your work. It creates a rhythm of harmony and joy. It keeps you curious, interested, and focused on your work.

One of my favorite "Peanuts" cartoon strips was one where Charlie Brown was hanging his head low. He was depressed. While his head was down and his shoulders were slumped over, he was explaining to Linus that if you want to be depressed, it's really important to look depressed; that your negative posture actually helps you remain low. He went on to correctly explain that if you were to lift your head up and smile, it would take you out of your depression and make you feel better!

The idea of whistling while you work is identical, only it's on the opposite end of the attitudinal spectrum. When you appreciate the privilege of doing whatever you are doing, it makes it virtually impossible to feel down. Instead of complaining, you'll notice all the things you love about your work and your life. When your attitude is positive, your perspective is heightened. You will focus less on the irritations and annoyances of your work and more on the aspects that are delightful and nurturing. Your curiosity will encourage you to see new options and new ways of doing things. It will keep your thinking fresh and spontaneous, alive and interesting. The people around you will be affected, too. They will be more likely to offer you genuine, positive feedback. They will actually listen to what you have to say and they will appreciate you more than ever before.

So much of what you've always wanted will emerge—and it all begins with a smile.

Starting today, see if you can incorporate a "whistle while you work" attitude into your daily routine. You'll notice an immediate shift from grumpy and serious to lighthearted and joyful. The creation of abundance is a joyful process. Lighten up and have some fun!

61.

ENCOURAGE CREATIVITY IN OTHERS
AND HAVE FAITH IN THEM

You'd be amazed at what people can (and will) do if you not only give them a chance but also believe in their potential. It's important to know that everyone has unique gifts and talents. It's your job to assist in bringing those gifts and talents out into the world. In other words, rather than sitting back and waiting for people to be perfect—and being frustrated when they are not—take some responsibility in the process by creating an ideal psychological working environment.

There's an old motto in business: Give someone a reputation to live up to and watch them shine. It's really true. Most people, given the right environment, are hard-working, talented, creative, and productive. They want to please others just as you and I want to. Unfortunately, however, most people are hardly ever exposed to an ideal working environment.

What happens to someone when she is insecure, resentful, or frightened? Very simply, she loses most of her motivation to please you as well as most of her other positive work-related qualities. Consider the following example: You have an assistant. Every day when he walks in the door, you remind him how incompetent he is. You point out his weaknesses and flaws. You belittle him in front of other people. Then you walk out the door. The question is, How does your assistant feel? It's hard to know for sure, because people react differently to the same set of facts. But it's a good bet that he's either frightened, insecure, resentful of you, or, most likely, all of the above. His job performance is going to be suspect. If you are disappointed in *him*, you are missing the point! In my book, you haven't done *your* job.

Wouldn't you increase your odds of securing a dedicated, hard-working assistant if you treated him with enormous, genuine respect? Wouldn't your assistant be more likely to work hard and keep your best interests in mind if you were to treat him with kindness, reminding him frequently how much you appreciate him, pointing out to him when he does something right? Ideally, we want everyone to feel good about themselves. We want others to believe in themselves, to feel confident and secure; to feel as if they are talented, competent, and creative. This way, everyone wins.

When you encourage creativity in others and have faith in them, it's analogous to creating the ideal conditions for a garden. You are "planting the seeds" for an environment where success is most likely to occur. When you plant a garden, you want to have the right type of soil, moisture, and sunshine. When you build people up—instead of pushing them down—you create the psychological equivalent. The same principle applies whether you are hiring a housekeeper, an attorney, an accountant, a publicist, or anyone else. It also applies to your children, your spouse, your friends, and your neighbors. It always works: When you believe in someone and when that person knows that you believe in her, magical things can happen. From this point on, see if you can expect great things from people. Do your part by creating the ideal working conditions. Be kind, patient, and supportive. Then, sit back and watch what happens.

62.

DON'T GIVE AWAY YOUR POWER

A major mistake made by many is to give away one's power to perceived experts. We do it all the time—to our doctors, financial planners, insurance salesmen. The assumption is: This person is an expert; I'd better listen to her. And, of course, sometimes this assumption is true and you should listen. But be careful to reserve the ultimate decision making for yourself. Always remember, if *you're* going to make money, *you* must take charge. Abundance and joy come from within you, not from other people.

As usual, the reason we so readily give our power away to others is fear. We worry that if we don't listen to an "expert," then we will surely be making a big mistake. Once you eliminate this fear, you'll realize that the creation of abundance is easier than you thought possible. When you make decisions from a place of wisdom rather than from a place of fear—and when you hold on to your own power—your decisions are usually good ones. They take you in directions that lead you toward your dreams and goals. It's a good idea to surround yourself with experts and to understand where your knowledge and experience is limited. However, the power should remain with you.

Suppose your insurance salesperson insists that what you really need is a million dollars of "whole life" coverage. But you plead with him that "Doing so will take most of my extra income and won't leave anything left for the investments I'd like to make." You go on to explain, "If I bought term insurance instead of whole life, I would have the same coverage at a tiny fraction of the cost." Your insurance salesperson, however, is grounded in fear and is trained to convince you to see life from his perspective. He believes he is giving you unbiased advice and is working in your best interest. "You'll regret it," he insists, attempting to reinforce any fear you may already be experiencing. What now? He is, after all, an "expert."

Whether you are dealing with a pushy insurance salesperson, a timid financial planner, an incompetent physician or attorney, or anyone else, the most relevant and important question to ask yourself is, Who is in charge here? The answer is *you*! Obviously, you want to take into consideration the advice you are getting, especially if you're paying for it. However, always remember that you are the boss. The ultimate decision is yours. Trust in your own instincts and wisdom, and not in the words and fears of experts. If you have a strong sense that your own instincts are the way to go, follow them. Trust yourself.

I went to a doctor once because I was feeling agitated a great deal of the time. The doctor *immediately* assumed that what I needed was antianxiety medicine. I felt this was utter nonsense! I insisted that it must be something else. "Listen here young man," he said in an arrogant tone, "I've seen this a thousand times." His obvious belief was "I know what's best for you! I'm the doctor. You're just the patient." I refused to accept his advice. I knew it must be something else. So I went to a more holistically inclined physician. After about two minutes of asking me questions about my lifestyle, he started to laugh. "Richard, " he said in a respectful and gentle tone, "you're drinking about ten times the amount of coffee you should be. Cut way back on your caffeine consumption and give me a call in about two weeks."

It turned out he was absolutely right. But more important than his good advice was the fact that I listened to my own instincts. Had I simply gone along with the first doctor's advice, I may have been on antianxiety medicine for the rest of my life, while drinking fifteen to twenty cups of coffee per day! My advice to you is this: Don't give away your power. You'll be amazed at the power of your own wisdom.

63.

CHARGE WHAT YOU ARE WORTH

An acquaintance of mine is one of the best professionals in her field. Virtually everyone she works with seems to agree. Why then does she charge between 30 and 40 percent less than her less experienced, less skilled competitors? Her problem, of course, is fear. She is unrealistically worried that, if she charges more, she will lose her clientele and her reputation as a fair businessperson. She believes, as many others do, that the primary reason she is so successful is because of her "reasonable" rates. Nonsense! The reason she is so successful in keeping a full clientele is because she's good at what she does. The truth is, she could probably *double* her fee and keep the vast majority of her clients. There's an old saying that applies not only to the sales of products but to the underpricing of services as well: If you're losing a penny per transaction, you can't make it up in volume.

Undercharging for professional services creates some serious, often unrealized problems. Perhaps the most serious of these is that undercharging keeps your schedule falsely overbooked, thus prohibiting you from having the time and energy to engage in other activities that may work to your greatest advantage—activities that could help create the abundance you desire.

Let's do some simple math. My friend, for example, works on average with six clients a day, six days a week. When you include set up, driving, scheduling, insurance, billing, and other factors, each client takes almost two hours of her time. Realistically, she needs all of her income to make ends meet. Her goal, about which she has been procrastinating for many years, is to go back to school. But, she complains, "I have no time." My argument is that she has it backwards! She doesn't have time *not* to go back to school. This is her dream. Abundance, of course, comes from following your dreams.

Let's assume, for argument's sake, that she doubled her fee from (symbolically) $50 to $100. And let's assume that raising her fee did, in fact, push some of her clients away. To illustrate the point, let's assume a worst-case scenario and that a full 50 percent of her clients left her practice! Look at what would happen: First, she would be making exactly the same amount of money in exactly half the time! Instantly, with one worry-free decision, she would have created the time to pursue her dream of going back to school! But wait, it gets even better. The clients that did stay with her would be the ones who were able to afford her higher fees. Thus, the people that *they* referred to her business would in all likelihood also be able to afford her services. She would be setting in motion an entirely new way of perceiving her work; a perception that would allow her to enjoy her work without worry or resentment, continue to provide a valuable service to her clients, *and* allow her the freedom and joy to pursue her dreams.

I am not advocating lofty pricing practices or greed. Neither am I suggesting that it's always appropriate and/or necessary to raise your prices. I have found, however, that because of fear and worry, many people *under*price their services and/or products. Unfortunately, this can set you up for failure by creating unnecessary demands on your time and energy—making you look and feel very busy but with very little of this energy going toward the creation of abundance. My suggestion is to charge what you are truly worth. This realistic yet confident pricing strategy keeps you free from resentment and pointed toward your dreams.

64.

LISTEN, REALLY LISTEN

Looking back on my life, I'm a little embarrassed to admit that I have been a poor listener. And while I'm a better listener today than I was five years ago, I still have a long way to go. As I look (and listen) to those around me, however, I feel like I have a lot of company.

People love to be listened to. So much so, in fact, that they will pay therapists enormous fees to listen to their stories and complaints. Consumers love to be listened to as well. They will happily pay top dollar for those people who are smart enough to understand that this is what they want—and what they demand. Unfortunately, only a tiny percentage of business persons do understand, or are willing to implement, this important notion.

What does your customer or client really want? Do you know? Are you guessing? Have you asked? If you *have* asked, are you giving her what she wants? Or are you giving her what *you* think she wants or needs? The difference in how you answer these questions may well be the difference between success and failure.

An interesting and eye-opening exercise is this: Pretend that you are a therapist. Listen very carefully to what your customer is saying. Ask probing questions like, What do you really want? and What would make you even happier with this product or service? Be genuine and listen like you've never listened before. Listen from your heart. Make it absolutely clear to your customer that the *only* thing that matters to you is that she is happy and that she is getting exactly what she wants and expects.

If you are running a small restaurant, for example, ask your customers if they would be willing to sit down with you for five minutes. Tell them you want to find out what would make their dining experience a little nicer than it already is. Ask them what they like about your restaurant, what they don't like, why they come in, and so forth. Listen carefully and respectfully.

When you listen in this manner, you may be shocked at the positive response. When people feel that they are listened to, they also feel appreciated and valued. Feeling listened to is such a rare experience that when someone does feel listened to, they tend to tell others about it. When your listening ear is genuine, you'll create raving fans and customers who will love you and will want to do business with you. Listening is like a magic formula that turns ordinary people into loyal, happy customers. One final tip: If you're married and/or have children, the same principle applies. If you want a closer relationship with your spouse or kids, the best place to start is by becoming a better listener!

65.

CULTIVATE HUMOR AND LEARN TO SMILE

Are you as amazed as I am at all the sourpusses out there in the "real world"? A lot of people have lost their perspective and take life so dreadfully seriously. Everything is a really big deal. On the other hand, once in a while you run into someone who is simply a delight. A person who has cultivated a sense of humor and hasn't forgotten how to smile.

This is undoubtedly one of the simplest suggestions in this entire book. Yet very few understand just how important it really is. So often, the difference between one business and another is negligible. In an external sense, it's almost impossible to tell the difference. The groceries and prices at one store are about the same as the one next door. The food at restaurant A is similar to that in restaurant B. The shoes in one establishment are the same ones you find in the store down the block. One example after another points to the simple truth that, in reality, products and services, on the surface and as a whole, look the same.

If I'm completely honest, I'd have to say that my buying decisions—the restaurants where I tend to eat, the places I purchase my clothes, the coffee shops I frequent, the stores I shop at—are virtually all made from the perspective of which employees are the friendliest, have the most genuine smiles and the nicest personalities. The coffee shops I go to are the ones that have the nicest people pouring the coffee. After all, the coffee tastes the same, it costs the same, the cups are the same, the atmosphere and locations are similar, but there is an enormous difference between waking up to a smiling, happy person, and, to use my seven-year-old daughter's words, waking up to "A serious little man." (This is what she calls me when I get too uptight!)

There is a small, family-owned grocery store in our town that is a beneficiary of this philosophy. The owner is one of the nicest men I've ever met. My kids actually *ask* if we can go to his store, and often we do. There is nothing in his store that we can't get elsewhere—and probably less expensively—but we really prefer to visit him. He has a beautiful smile and both my daughters, as well as myself, deeply appreciate it. Over the years he has earned thousands of dollars of our business simply by having a genuine smile. There is no amount of advertising or anything else he could have done to earn our business. His marketing strategy is effective and free! Believe it or not, the same is true, to some degree, when we choose a doctor, accountant, housekeeper, or other professional. Obviously, we want and need competent people to work for us. However, all things being equal (and they often are), what people want is someone who is nice to be around. I've actually avoided certain doctors, especially pediatricians, when they act like "serious little men." I simply don't want my kids to be around that kind of energy unless I have no other options. Why not choose someone who is competent *and* happy?

The benefits of a sense of humor and a nice smile to you extend far beyond greater profits. You'll also have the privilege of feeling better yourself and making others happy as well. I believe that smiling actually gives you more energy, and perhaps even better health. So lighten up and smile. Your payback will be immediate and significant.

66.

START A BUYERS CLUB

This strategy is a fun one—plus, you'll save a lot of time and a great deal of money.

There are many discount bulk-buying warehouses in the country, and indeed throughout the entire world. They have practically everything you and your family could possibly need in the way of bulk-item groceries, household goods, items for your car, gifts, jewelry, other assorted things, and, to a lesser extent, even books.

They have the unbelievable advantage of buying from their suppliers in enormous bulk. They buy everything from watches and television sets to ice cream and canned soup, in quantities you would not believe. You, as a consumer, can take advantage of their enormous discounts by purchasing in large quantities yourself.

So, what's the drawback? The only one I can think of is that most of us don't really need and/or don't want to fill our homes with so many items at once. In other words, while we may need paper towels, we may not have the space, or want to put out the money up front (even though it's far cheaper in the long run), to buy forty rolls of paper towels at once. Enter: The Buying Club.

By setting up your own buying club you'll get the best of all possible worlds. Gather together three or more friends (you can even go as high as eight people—more if you drive a bus), and create your own buying club. The way the club works is remarkably simple. And if it's done correctly, you can save thousands of dollars each year on your shopping bill. You'll also spend far less time at the grocery store, thus leaving you more time for other, more important things.

For our purposes here, let's assume you create a club with just four members. Each month, one member acts as the buyer. The other members submit their shopping lists a day or two before the shopping day and send or give them to the buyer. Some clubs also turn into an excuse for a social gathering. In these cases, the members might get together once a month for lunch the day before the shopping trip (at the buyer's home, for example), and create their shopping lists, exchange money and so forth, in addition to having a good time. On the day of the trip, the buyer goes out and gets everything on everyone's list. Again, because most items are purchased in such huge quantities, the overall price is far less than it would be if all the members went out and shopped for themselves.

It's a near perfect system. In our example here, you would only be required to go shopping three times each year—a small price to pay for all the money you'll save. I encourage you to explore this idea. It's really easy to implement, and it will save you lots of money. Who knows, maybe with all the money you save, you'll go out and start a new business or invest in something that will take off like a rocket.

67.

BUILD UP A LARGE "TRUST FUND"

I don't know about you, but I grew up believing that only very wealthy (usually spoiled) people had the privilege and security of a "trust fund." Not true! Each individual—every one of us—has the kind of trust fund that really matters: the trust of other people. The only question is, How large is it? Many people, not knowing how important a trust fund is to their own success, are practically bankrupt in this critical account. Yet others, intuitively aware of its importance, are rich in this category beyond their wildest dreams. Sooner or later, a large trust fund will pay enormous dividends toward your creation of abundance. There is a direct correlation between the size of your trust fund and the desire and willingness of others to work with and help you.

The way to build a large trust fund is simple and straightforward. It involves being accountable for your actions, however large or small, doing what you say you are going to do, delivering on your promises, being on time, and so forth. Anything and everything you do that reinforces your own trustworthiness is like money in the bank. Accountability is derived in both small and large doses. For example, if you tell someone you are going to call them at three o'clock, or pick them up at the airport, and you do so on time, as you say you are going to do, you earn small credits toward your trust fund. Likewise, if you tell someone that you'll send them a copy of a book you've been discussing, and you actually do it, you earn credibility with that person. If you *don't* do exactly what you say you're going to do, while any individual action or inaction may not seem like a very big deal, it decreases your credibility and *reduces* the size of your trust fund. I know people, for example, who will make small promises about

151

things they are going to do practically every time I speak to them. While these are nice, decent people with good intentions, and while nothing they're promising is all that important, they usually don't deliver what they say they are going to deliver. The sad result of this nonaccountability is that I have learned to expect them to renege. In other words, while I may really like them as people, I don't necessarily *trust* them, nor do I take them very seriously. In all likelihood, other people don't either.

Obviously, no one is perfect. We all make mistakes, renege on commitments, show up late, and occasionally forget appointments. I have learned, however, that it's far easier and wiser to avoid making commitments I can't keep than it is to make promises, however small, that may eventually reduce the size of my trust fund.

Starting today, speak and behave with your trust fund in mind. Before you say you are going to do something that someone else is going to depend on, check in with yourself. Ask yourself, Will I be able to keep this commitment? Remember, the size of your trust fund depends on it.

68.

SELL THE SIZZLE, NOT THE STEAK

In any business, it's critical to know what you're actually selling. Very often it's not what it appears to be. If you're selling a house, for example, you're obviously *not* selling wood, brick, or concrete. Instead, you're tapping into a person's dream—his or her perception of how they are going to feel and live once they get into the home.

A good friend of mine was the first to teach me this valuable lesson. He used to own a beautiful apartment complex in a lovely California town. Once, while I was in town, he gave me a tour of the property. It was complete with tennis courts, two beautiful swimming pools, a workout room, and a picnic area. "Wow," was my reaction. "I'll bet everyone loves to use all this great stuff." "Actually, Richard, you may be shocked to know that virtually no one uses the facilities. I wish they would, but the reality is, they don't," was his response. It turned out that less than 10 percent of the residents had *ever* used any of the facilities! And less than 5 percent used them regularly. This came as quite a shock to me as I was always a person who would fall into that 5 percent.

My friend went on to explain that, despite the fact that almost no one uses the facilities, virtually everyone, before they move in, *thinks* they are going to. In fact, it's one of the primary reasons they choose an apartment complex, and one of the only reasons they are willing to pay top dollar for it. The "steak," in this example, is the apartment complex. The "sizzle" is the fancy surroundings and facilities—the sizzle is what's doing the selling, not the steak. So the best way to sell a potential resident on the property was for my friend to be sure to show everyone the complete facilities. Invariably, this would get his potential customers dreaming of how they were going to finally take time to relax, learn to play tennis, swim in the pool, enjoy barbecues with friends, and so forth.

The analogy of selling the sizzle instead of the steak can be extended to many other types of businesses. I have to admit that, often, I've made my decision on which hotel to stay at based solely on the fact that they have an indoor pool and room service. Rarely, however, do I actually take advantage of these luxuries. The same is true with restaurants. Once in a while my wife and I will choose a restaurant because they have an incredible dessert menu—we dream of that decadent piece of chocolate cake—but, except for an extremely rare occasion, we will usually pass on dessert. We either feel too full after the meal or worry about the weight we are going to gain should we choose to eat it. The point is, we enter the restaurant not because of any rational thinking but because we, like most people, are influenced by our thoughts and dreams.

Think of the millions of exercise gadgets that are sold each year. Surveys show that everyone absolutely believes that they are going to become disciplined and use the equipment on a regular basis. New customers dream of flat stomachs and muscular arms. However, statistics show us that 90 percent of consumers stop using the equipment within ten days of purchasing it—and virtually all the rest quit after a month or two. Only a tiny percentage of people continue to use the equipment. The companies making these products know that the best way to sell these machines is to effectively tap into the dreams of the consumer. So they put photographs of beautiful, muscular woman and firm, physically fit handsome men on the boxes. The "sizzle" is the possibility that you and I might look like those people in the photograph.

It's important to know that people love to dream. So if you want to sell something, be sure you know what the dreams are. Factor this knowledge into whatever it is you are selling—product or service—and you'll be amazed at how much more effective you will become.

69.

GO AHEAD AND DO IT

I have discovered an amazing secret that works remarkably well. The secret can be summed up in a single sentence that is also the title of Susan Jeffers' wonderful book: *Feel the Fear and Do It Anyway*! I've found that, remarkably, virtually every time I'm really frightened to do something I need to do, and I go ahead and do it anyway, that it almost always turns out okay. It passes. In other words, somehow, despite my worry, I *do* get through it. I always come out the other end. I always survive. What's more, it's almost never as difficult as I make it out to be. In fact, it's usually far easier.

It's very helpful to remind yourself that, despite your fears, here you are. Somehow you have managed to survive it all. In this sense, all your worries have been a mirage—a waste of time, irrelevant.

Think of all the times you've lost sleep over something you had to do. Perhaps you were anticipating a job interview or peer review. Maybe you had a difficult job to do—you had to fire someone or give him bad news. You fretted and worried, sometimes for days, even weeks. But in spite of all the worry, you managed to get through it. In the past, whether you lost your job, felt humiliated, faced a difficult challenge, or whatever else, here you are. You survived. This doesn't mean you haven't had difficult things to do—we all do—but it does mean that the worry we experience is nothing more than a mental irritant. When we set it aside, we can get on with our lives, including our many challenges.

In my career I've felt frightened many times. I've had to speak in front of large audiences and in front of cameras, despite being a very shy person. I've had to create interesting articles and books, after practically flunking high school English. I've faced deadlines that I felt were unreasonable, even impossible to meet. And yes, I worried about it all. Yet when I look back, I realize that, despite the mental anguish I put myself through, I always did get through the situation, one way or another, whatever it may have been. Usually, I'm able to rise to the occasion, and I'll bet you are, too.

There's a lesson here for all of us: We're stronger than our fears and more competent than our worries. The next time you find yourself worrying, step back for a moment and reflect on past worries. Doesn't it seem all too familiar? Is it possible that you're merely repeating a mental exercise? Do you think the worry is going to help? Aren't you going to do whatever you're worried about anyway? What's the point of the worry? I think these are really important questions. And I believe that if you take the time to reflect on them, you'll agree that if you "feel the fear and do it anyway," all will be well. And once you get the hang of it, the worries begin to go away.

70.

BE WILLING TO TAKE ADVICE

Generally speaking, people don't take advice, even good advice. This is true even when the advice is free and when it's offered with love. Think about yourself. How often do you really, honestly take someone else's advice? How often do you say to yourself, or out loud, "That's a great idea. That's a much better way of doing it than the way I have been doing it." This type of humility is almost unheard of in our culture, yet think about the wisdom here. In order to grow, we need to see things differently. We don't want to do the same things over and over if they're not working well. Instead, we want to open our eyes to new and improved ways of doing things. But how can we see things differently if we refuse to take to heart the suggestions from others? It seems so obvious.

Sometimes, the reason we don't take advice is pure stubbornness. We want to do things our own way—even if it's not working! Other times, we avoid advice out of fear. We might be frightened that we're going to look bad in the eyes of someone else, or that we're going to seem incompetent. Or we might be fearful that the advice we get isn't going to help— that if *we* can't figure it out, then no one else can either. Sometimes we've received bad advice or too much advice, and we vow to not repeat that same mistake.

My suggestion in this area is simple and straightforward: Take the advice. Life is so much simpler when you involve the strengths and expertise of others. After all, if you absolutely knew what to do to make your life better or more successful, you'd be doing it already. But if you're struggling in any aspect of your life (and we all do), you need advice.

I'm certain that one of the primary reasons I've had some degree of success in my life is my absolute willingness to seek out, listen to, and often take advice. This makes life so easy that, occasionally, it doesn't seem fair. I love to get advice, especially from competent people. I believe that if someone has worked hard, achieved some measure of success, and is willing to help, I'd be a fool *not* to listen! Plus, as you probably already know, almost everyone loves to give advice. By listening to someone and actually taking their advice, you not only get good results but you also get to contribute to the joy of another person.

Unfortunately, many people miss out on one of the surest shortcuts to success: taking advice. So often, when a person struggles, he or she is very close to a major breakthrough. They are literally "an inch away" from achieving their goals and dreams. If they would just open their eyes to a blind spot, see something they are doing in a slightly different or new way, their success would be phenomenal and certain. I have friends and family members who fall into this category. I believe they are incredibly talented people, on the verge of possible greatness, or on the verge of improving their life in a meaningful way. Yet this one tiny flaw—the unwillingness to listen to anyone else and the absolute unwillingness to take advice—consistently gets in their way. Don't let this minor obstacle get in your way. The advice is out there. People want to help you. Allow yourself to receive help and the quality of your life will soar.

71.

ASK YOURSELF, WHAT HAVE I CONTRIBUTED
TO THIS PROBLEM?

Many people rarely, if ever, ask this critical question. Instead, they automatically assume that any problem they are having must be someone else's fault. If there is a disagreement or argument, it's the other person's fault. If something went wrong, someone else made a mistake. If there's a glitch in the schedule, "someone else must have dropped the ball." It simply never occurs to many people that something is their fault. Or, at the very least, that they may be partly responsible.

On the surface, it might seem nice to believe that you're never to blame. The problem, however, with this "never blame me" philosophy is that you'll rarely be able to pinpoint the one aspect of problem solving that is truly solvable: your own contribution. Once you eliminate the fear associated with admitting that you are, at times, responsible for the parts of your life that aren't working—minor annoyances *and* larger problems— you open a whole new door of possibilities.

Once you're willing to accept responsibility for the problems in your life, you will see obvious solutions that take very minor adjustments to change. Sometimes there's a fine line between doing something really well and doing something really badly. Often, the solution is to simply change something you are doing.

It's really not all that helpful to contemplate the faults and contributions to problems of others. Rarely can you do anything about other people and the way they handle things. It's simple, however (unless you're too frightened), to make changes in your own responses. I try, whenever I can, to see where *I'm* contributing. If, for example, I'm frustrated with the way a business relationship is progressing, I take a look at the way I'm treating that person. I ask myself questions like, Am I being too pushy or demanding? Am I assuming that he or she really understands what I'm asking when they may not? Am I being unclear or unfair? These types of questions are helpful for two reasons. First, I'm almost *always* able to see some contribution on my end. Second, when I do, I can usually make a simple adjustment that can actually help the situation.

Just last week, for example, I was frustrated with someone I was working with over the phone. She was working for me, but nothing seemed to be happening. I was impatient and kept pushing her to perform. Then it occurred to me that she might be angry at me for pushing too hard. I realized that I was terribly overcommitted myself and was, without knowing it, expecting her to operate at my crazy pace. When I called to sincerely apologize, I could sense her relaxation over the phone. I backed off and, as I did, her performance began to improve. Had I continued to blame her for a problem I was clearly contributing to, she would have remained resentful and, in all likelihood, would have continued to perform well beneath her capacity. We both would have ended up losers in the deal.

Obviously, I'm not suggesting that everything is your fault, or that you should spend an exorbitant amount of time and energy thinking about your faults and drawbacks. To do so would be a different type of negative habit. It's critical, however, that you're honest about your contribution to your problems. Don't bury your head in the sand. If you truly want to excel in your life, you must be willing to look in the mirror and, with humility and honesty, reflect on your contributions to what's not going right in your life. That way, you can do something about it.

72.

CONSIDER THAT WISDOM MAY BE
EVEN MORE IMPORTANT THAN IQ

All things being equal, intelligence is a wonderful quality to possess. However, if you had to choose between the two, I'd say that wisdom is even more important than intelligence in your quest for joy and abundance. There are many highly intelligent people who fail to use their intelligence to best advantage. There are also many extremely intelligent people who live very unhappy lives. Sadly, in many cases, it seems that you can fit the wisdom of a highly intelligent person into a tiny thimble.

While you could rank order people in terms of their IQ, the number you assigned to a person would say nothing about their degree of success or happiness. Despite this fact, however, as a society, we continue to revere intelligence, yet barely even stop to consider wisdom at all.

Unlike intelligence, wisdom is a quality that you cannot accurately measure. It's invisible. It includes aspects of life such as perspective, spontaneity, creativity, and social skills. Wisdom is your sense of knowing, an intuitive feeling. William James, often thought of as the "father of modern psychology," said, "Wisdom is seeing something in a nonhabitual manner." It's seeing an old problem in a new, fresh light. As you discover and begin to trust your wisdom, you'll free yourself from your fixed and habitual patterns of thinking and problem solving, and will more easily be able to navigate yourself toward joy and prosperity. In a nutshell, wisdom is the ability to "see" an answer without having to "think" of an answer. It exists outside the confines of your thinking mind. Often, wisdom is seeing the obvious. And unlike the thinking mind, wisdom contains no worry.

One of my favorite stories that demonstrates wisdom is about a giant truck that gets stuck under an overpass. The truck was too tall for the available clearance. The police called out the best, brightest, and most expensive engineers in the city to try to figure out what to do. They brought along their computers, clip boards, and slide rules. They discussed the issue amongst themselves. They racked their brains for hours. They simply couldn't figure out how to remove the truck without damaging the freeway above. It all seemed so complicated. Then a small boy, about seven years old, walked up to the men and tugged on one of their pants legs. "Excuse me, sir," the little boy said in a respectful tone. "Why don't you just let the air out of the tires?" Out of the mouths of babes the problem was solved.

The people who have made the most money, or who have been the most successful in their careers, are certainly not always the most intelligent or the most highly educated. There are plenty of Harvard graduates who have a very difficult time making any significant money, despite their incredible education. Usually, the people who make the most money and who have the most fun doing so are highly creative, highly motivated, have great intuition, solid gut reactions and instincts, and/or the ability to see opportunities. These qualities, and others, stem not so much from intelligence but from wisdom. This is *not* an argument against formal education, or against standard intelligence. Yet it's critical to be aware that you don't need to use any lack of formal education as ammunition against yourself. Education is important and helpful. But don't let anyone convince you that if you aren't formally educated, you are doomed to failure—because you're not.

The best way to access your wisdom is simply to know that it exists and to trust in it. Keep your mind as clear as possible, know that a deeper, more intelligent type of thinking—your wisdom—is available. When you feel that your thinking is too frenetic, overactive, or that you are trying too hard, experiment with backing off. You will find that a softer focus and less effort, not more, will usually result in a better use of the mind. Relax and succeed.

73.

ELIMINATE THE WORDS "I'M NOT A SALESPERSON"
FROM YOUR VOCABULARY

Yes, you are! If you have something—anything—to offer someone else, then you are, at least partially, a salesperson. If you ever even attempt to get another person to purchase, try, or even look at what you're offering, then you *are* a salesperson. And that's okay. The point here is that selling is an important part of the web of life. It's okay to sell. It doesn't make you a bad person.

Many people have a self-destructive attitude toward selling, treating it like a four-letter word, thus creating a wall between themselves and their own success. Rather than accepting the fact that we all have something to sell—our time, energy, ideas, products, vision, dreams, or services—they choose to deny the fact that they have anything to do with selling. I have seen this silly belief interfere with virtually every type of business venture, from network marketing to personal service businesses, to running a bakery. Whenever you set yourself up as a person who is against selling, you create a difficult environment to succeed.

The bigger the deal you make out of it, the more you interfere, energetically, with your own success. Keep in mind that your energy follows your attention. If your attention is busy being a nonsalesperson, all that will happen is that you will become ineffective at selling—even though you are selling. Thus, any attempt to convince yourself that you aren't selling anything is counterproductive and unwise.

74.

CONSIDER THAT BUSYNESS GETS IN YOUR WAY

Tom Hanks, one of the best actors of our time, was being interviewed on television when he responded to a question by saying, "More isn't always better." He was attempting to get across the message that busyness gets in your way, that too many things going on at once, too many projects or details to attend to, can be a distraction that keeps us from being our best; when your head is too full, there's little room left for freshness and creativity. He is absolutely right!

Many of us are so busy that we lose sight of which end is up. We rush around, looking and feeling very busy, but, in actuality, we are getting very little of substance done. Our creativity and wisdom are lost in our busyness. We lose sight of what's truly relevant and most important. New ideas are hard to come by.

Often, in business decisions, a single moment of thoughtful reflection is all that is needed to make the best possible choice. However, if you are too busy, scrambling around, frantic, you'll often miss that precious, all-important moment. You'll see all the chaos, but you won't see the obvious solutions. For example, I met a real estate buyer who purchases properties that others had attempted, but failed, to renovate and resell at a profit. He told me that, in most cases, the failure was the result of acting too impulsively with a very busy mind. "You see," said this successful businessman, as he pointed to a project he was working on, "all this property really needed was a cosmetic tune up. The people who owned it before me went broke trying to make it perfect. There were indeed a lot of problems with the property, but they weren't nearly as serious as they believed them to be. They were rushing around so frantically that they lost sight of the obvious."

Somewhere along the line, most of us got the message that looking, acting, and being really busy is a virtue. Certainly there are times when we truly are busy and can't do much about it. Ironically, however, when we stop worrying so much about getting everything done; when we stop looking and telling others how busy we are, we are better able to determine what's most important. We calm down and see what really needs to be done.

A critical aspect of success is to schedule time in your day when absolutely nothing is going on. Even if you can only spare a few extra minutes a day, you need to have "down time." Rather than overlapping your meetings and appointments, and running them together, see if you can allow a little extra time. Create some space. Stop worrying that you won't get everything done. What you'll find is that when you have a little more space for yourself and a little less hurry, many of your best ideas will begin to surface. This has certainly proven to be the case for me. Most of my best ideas come not when I'm overwhelmed in my busyness, but during the moments between the busyness when I have a few quiet moments to myself and my wisdom has a chance to surface. Starting today, see if you can become a little less "busy." You'll be surprised at what occurs to you.

75.

THINK ABOUT PURPLE SNOWFLAKES

I'll bet you read that sentence twice. Of course, that's the whole idea—to get your attention. I've found that many people are a little timid, even frightened, to stand out, to do things a little differently. They worry about what people are going to think, or what they are going to say, or that their efforts will be perceived as foolish, or that they won't really work. In marketing, however, the whole idea is to get someone, or a group of people, to take a look at what you're selling, asking for, or offering.

The notion of purple snowflakes is a metaphor for standing out in the crowd. In our world of incredible competition and sheer volume, it's more important than ever to stand apart. You certainly don't want to fade into the background. As long as the product or service you are marketing is at least as good as everyone else's, standing out—offering purple snowflakes—will often make the difference.

When I really want someone to open the mail I'm sending them, for example, I send it via Federal Express or some other overnight delivery service. Obviously, this is a much more expensive route, but think about the tradeoff for a moment. Suppose you're sending a request to a famous and/or super-busy person who receives dozens of requests each day. If you, like virtually everyone else, simply send your request in a regular business envelope, the chances are excellent that it will be days, perhaps even weeks, before the person even opens your letter. Yet very few people, irrespective of how famous or busy they are, can resist opening an overnight delivery package. Now that they have opened your mail, there's a chance they will respond favorably. In this case, your "purple snowflake" was the Federal

Express package itself. I can assure you that if your request is granted, you'll be sold on the idea of purple snowflakes.

A friend of mine, in my eyes a marketing genius, wanted to get an ex-professional football player to invest in his business. The business was solid and an excellent opportunity. The problem was that this particular ex-athlete, known in part for the wealth he had been able to amass, was approached by all sorts of credible entrepreneurs on a daily basis. It was fairly common knowledge that he had essentially stopped reading the request letters.

My friend, adept at creating purple snowflakes, wanted to overcome this obstacle because he knew that if he could just get the athlete to read his reports, that he would seriously consider the investment opportunity. So here's what he did: He taped his request to an actual NFL football and sent it to the man. Needless to say, the former football star recognized the shape of the package, was curious, and opened it immediately. Within a few days my friend received a personal call—not from a secretary, from the athlete himself—congratulating him on his incredible creativity. The athlete asked my friend to dinner, telling him that, as long as the numbers checked out, and everything was ethical, as it seemed to be, he would be honored to do business with someone who was so clever.

Obviously, not every purple snowflake is going to be so well received. But instead of giving up, and without becoming obnoxious about it, see if you can create another purple snowflake. Drop your fears about how your snowflakes will be received. As they say in Hollywood, any attention is better than no attention.

76.

STAY OUT OF REVERSE

Reverse, in a psychological sense, works the same as the reverse gear in your car—it takes you backward. And, like your car, if you want to change direction and begin moving forward, you must shift gears completely. It's impossible to move forward in reverse gear.

The way reverse sounds in day-to-day living is this: "Can you believe what happened yesterday? Those guys were jerks. Every time I work on something, it gets messed up. That's the sixth time this week our deliveries were delayed. I'm still mad at what she said to me." There are an unlimited number of possible examples. Anytime you are fixated, immobilized, absorbed in, or even overly concerned with something that is over—whether it happened this morning or ten years ago—constitutes reverse gear. I challenge you to take an honest look at how often you (and probably most people you know), are focused in reverse. You may be shocked.

The way you can tell if you are in reverse gear is simple. It will feel heavy and serious. You won't be moving forward; you might even be moving backward. You'll be stagnant, stuck in emotional quicksand. You'll be making references to the past, to yesterday, last week, last year, or to your childhood. You'll be complaining about things, people, circumstances, events, rules, problems, and concerns that are, for the most part, over and done with. Being in reverse saps the joy out of whatever you are doing. It's boring, unforgiving, and counterproductive.

The reason people find it so difficult to get out of reverse gear is that they can so easily justify being there. In other words, they argue for their "right" to be in reverse by saying things like, "But he *did* sabotage the deal," or "She *did* criticize me in public." People will use the fact that

171

events actually took place as evidence to support their anger and frustration. What they usually fail to see, however, is that right now, in *this* moment, the event they are frustrated about is over. The only factor keeping it alive is their memory, their own thinking.

Obviously, it's important to learn from our past, from our mistakes. I can assure you, however, that being in reverse gear will not help you do so. To learn from our past experiences, it's helpful to gently reflect on the way we have done things. Reverse gear isn't gentle. In fact, it's harsh.

The way *out* of reverse is to notice how it feels to be *in* reverse. If you can observe yourself—your mind, your thoughts, your attention—focused on past events, or past frustrations, you can gently bring your attention back to the present. Training your mind to stay out of reverse can be a little like training a puppy to stay at your side. The puppy will stay for a minute, then dart away. Your mind is like that, too. It can stay focused for a minute or two, then dart backward to an annoyance from this morning or a frustration from yesterday. The most effective way to train your puppy is to gently lead him back to your side. The same approach works with your mind as well. As you notice your thoughts drifting backward, remind yourself that the past is over and done with. Then, gently and easily, guide yourself back to the here and now. All it takes is a little patience and some practice. Pretty soon, your tendency to be in reverse gear will be a part of your past.

77.

LET GO OF THE FEAR THAT IF YOU'RE RELAXED OR HAPPY, YOU'RE GOING TO FAIL

I was recently interviewed on a radio station located in Cincinnati, Ohio. We were discussing my assertion that "sweating the small stuff" interferes not only with your sense of well-being but with your productivity as well. The two people—a man and a woman—conducting the interview were exceptionally confrontational and suspicious. I could sense a complete lack of joy and a very serious nature. Life, to them, was clearly an emergency. The gentleman, in particular, was convinced that if a person was to follow my "program," as he put it, they would surely become apathetic, if not homeless! "If you're not uptight," he insisted, "you'll lose your drive."

Sadly, many people believe that if you aren't uptight and serious, you are doomed to failure. In my entire lifetime, I've never been more convinced that something is not true. Let me give you an analogy:

Think back to last year's Thanksgiving dinner. Remember how you felt after eating all that food. If you're anything like most Americans who are privileged enough to enjoy a feast such as this, you were stuffed. And along with feeling stuffed, you felt tired. Am I right? When you eat too much, the energy that is usually directed toward normal body functions—healing, cell division, metabolism, and all sorts of other good stuff—must go toward digestion. This makes you feel sleepy and lethargic. You lose motivation and energy.

There is an emotional equivalent. You can extend this same metaphor to your tendency to be overly serious and immobilized over little things.

When you are angry, bothered, and annoyed, virtually all the mental and emotional energy that could otherwise be used for creativity, spontaneity, and mental ambition is taken away. When you focus on things that irritate you, like the gentleman who was interviewing me, it interferes with the process of creation. It keeps you down, stuck, focused not on the wonder and mystery of life and its many possibilities but on what's lacking, what's wrong, and all that makes you mad and frustrated.

To argue for, to even suggest that, going with the flow is the same as burying your head in the sand is, quite frankly, foolish. It's wrong. In fact, I've found the opposite is almost always true. As you lighten up, relax, and unwind, you open the doors of creativity and joy that were previously hidden. You discover new interests and new possibilities. So, starting today, remind yourself that it's okay to relax—in fact, it's more than okay, it's downright important.

78.

BE AWARE OF POSITIVE BURNOUT

Burnout is a major topic of conversation in the business world. We discuss it, dread it, and have theories about why it exists. Estimates are that seven out of ten of us feel burned out at any given time, and virtually everyone will experience burnout at some point in their career. The most common reaction to burnout, however, is our fear surrounding it. We worry and wonder, When will it happen to me?

But have you ever stepped back far enough to see the *positive* side of burnout? Often, burnout is a signal that something new, exciting, and profitable is just around the corner! After all, why would you make major changes in your life in the absence of these types of feelings? You probably wouldn't. If you always felt great about your career and current direction, you may spend the rest of your life doing the very same thing.

There was a time in my life when I thought I was going to make it as a professional tennis player. Yet after many years of aches and pains, as well as some noticeable shortcomings in my game, I began to feel burned out. Had it not been for these feelings, I surely would have continued on the same path, which included a great deal of struggle, frustration, and little chance of major success. If not for my burnout, I would have been missing out on a great education and a personally fulfilling career. As I look back on my life, I can see that virtually every positive fork in the road was preceded by a certain degree of burnout. And in retrospect, it was all positive burnout.

The point here is that it's not at all necessary to freak out or worry when you feel burned out. Instead, try to keep things in perspective. Remember that negative feelings can be deceptive. Often they are positive signals disguised as negative feelings. As you worry less, two things will happen. First, you'll discover that most burnout is nothing more than a bad mood taken too seriously. If you don't worry too much about it, it will probably go away and you'll regain your enthusiasm for your work within a short period of time. Second, the less you worry about burnout, the less energy you give it, the clearer you will be about any needed changes in your life. In other words, you'll know what to do.

Worry gets in the way of your wisdom and common sense. As you let go of fear, as you investigate your feelings of burnout, you may discover that your feelings are trying to tell you something, point you in a new direction, redirect your energy—or something else that is *positive* in nature. As you learn to trust your inner resources by letting go of fear, you'll discover that your wisdom will tell you exactly what you need to be doing at any given point in your life. Try putting a positive slant on your feelings of burnout and watch them fade away.

79.

DIVE IN

If you're going to do something important, the best time to start is right now. Not later, tomorrow, next week, next month, or next year. Right now. The best strategy is to "dive in." I know there's always an important reason to put off doing today what you are planning or hoping to do tomorrow. In fact, there are usually many good reasons to wait. Despite these good reasons, however, I urge you to get started now. The pure and simple fact is that the individuals who start *now*, who dive in, have a far better track record and enjoy much greater degrees of success than those who wait. They also tend to be more engaged in their lives and have a lot more fun.

About a year ago I attended a business meeting with my wife, Kris. There was a woman at the meeting who seemed to be bright, well educated, and talented. The purpose of the meeting was to help people get started in an exciting new business. This particular woman decided to wait. Despite being "certain" (her word) that she wanted to get involved, she wanted to "think about it" for a while. She wanted the time to be right.

A few months later, we attended a different meeting where my wife was one of the speakers. Who did we see? The same woman. We urged her to get started. "Not quite yet" was her response. She was "really committed" to the program but didn't want to "dive in" (again, her words). Well, the story continues and gets even worse. As of this writing, the woman still hasn't gotten started.

The good news is that several of the people who did get started at that first meeting are well on their way to building very successful businesses. They knew that the key was simply to get started and not to put it off.

These people, the ones who *did* get started, have the same obstacles, if not more, than the woman who hesitated. They have children to take care of, jobs to go to, responsibilities, bills, houses to keep clean, lawns to mow, trips to take, school plays and other family-oriented things to attend to, relatives to visit, new babies on the way, and everything else imaginable. The secret to success is to understand that, despite all of these responsibilities, the best time to begin is now.

You don't have to do everything in one day to succeed, but you do have to get started. Just getting off the ground, getting started, is, for most people, the most difficult part. Once you do, the rest will usually fall into place. If you are interested in, or considering, a new venture, as long as it's something that you are truly committed to, my advice is simple: dive in.

80.

JUST ONCE, TRY SOMETHING DIFFERENT

Many of us do the same things, day after day, for most of our adult lives. We have the same habits, go to the same places, hold the same opinions, get upset over the same things, think the same thoughts, meet with the same people, do things in the same way. And for the most part, we get the same results. How boring!

It took years for me to understand the obvious: If I keep doing the same things, making the same mistakes, and having the same expectations, I'm probably going to keep getting the same results as well as the same frustrations. I finally realized that if I wanted something different, something more, I was going to have to try something different. I did, and it worked. And I've seen it work over and over again for virtually everyone who is willing to try. Most people are stuck right where they are. The reason they're stuck, however, isn't usually due to circumstances, incompetence, or lack of opportunity, but a simple unwillingness to change, to try new things.

I'm not necessarily talking about trying a different job or career (although that might be a good idea, too). Instead, I'm referring here to smaller, inner changes that you can make on a day-to-day, moment-to-moment basis—changes in your attitude, reactions, and expectations. I'm talking about being willing to meet new people at new places, take new risks, and face old fears. Perhaps you can, for once, listen to someone else's opinion or read a periodical that you usually disagree with. Over and over again I hear people saying things like "I've always done things that way" or "That's just the type of person I am." These things are said as if they are carved in stone, as if there is something other than their own thinking and attitude that is holding them in place. There isn't. It's amazing what you can learn by simply opening your mind and trying new things.

Starting today, tell yourself that you are going to do something, however small, a little differently. Perhaps you can be more friendly to the people you work with. Maybe it's never occurred to you to invite your boss to lunch. Perhaps you've never stayed late or arrived early at the office. Maybe it's not too late to overcome your fear of asking others to help you, or for their advice. Whoever you are, whatever you do, there is always something you can do a little differently. Experiment with newness. You may find that you love the tiny changes you make and that you can open exciting new doors by making relatively small adjustments. Just once, try something different. If you're okay with the changes, which I suspect you will be, you might want to try some other changes as well.

81.

HELP SOMEONE ELSE SUCCEED

It's been said that the absolute best way to learn something is to try to teach it. I've found that not only is this assumption true, but that the learning curve I experience when I teach is often astounding. I have, for example, agreed to give a lecture to an entire student body of more than 3,500 people on a topic I was familiar with but was by no means an expert on. I knew, however, that by agreeing to teach others, I would force myself to "own" the material. Teaching others helps us pinpoint our knowledge and the way we express it. It also helps us to raise our standards of excellence by encouraging us to think in creative, articulate ways. Most of us want to practice in our own lives what we teach. So, if we teach someone how to be more successful, we will invariably help ourselves in the process.

There are probably many people in your life you are in a position to help. Perhaps you're an expert or very experienced in your field. Maybe there is someone who could use some feedback, advice, or encouragement. Could you possibly meet a younger, less experienced person for lunch or coffee? Is there someone in your immediate family or circle of friends who is struggling? If you look around, I'll bet you can find someone who would really appreciate your help.

I'm not suggesting that you overwhelm someone with your presence, or with your ideas. You don't have to change a person's life or get overly involved. Sometimes, all a person needs is a little jump start. A friend, for example, might need some help with a personal issue—quitting smoking or drinking. You can help them succeed in this goal by being a source of support or a good listener. Or you may have some clever marketing ideas for a friend starting or struggling in his or her small business. Your ideas could make the difference between that person quitting or helping them turn the corner. You can help them succeed.

My only word of caution is to be sure to get permission before offering your help. Be gentle and patient. Not everyone wants or is ready for help. And that's okay. Don't take it personally. Everyone is at a different place in their life.

As you help others succeed, even in very small ways, it helps you redefine and reflect on your own goals, assumptions, and ways of doing things. If you suggest to someone else, for example, that they think of education as a lifelong process, it might remind you that *you* haven't taken a class in years. I'm often amazed at how my advice applies to my own life and my own success. Just the other day, someone asked me for advice. Upon reflection, I suggested that he desperately needed a break or else he might burn out. That evening, I realized that I had been working way too hard and that *I* needed to slow down! I think you'll find that one of the shortcuts to success is to help others succeed.

82.

PERSEVERE

When I was just getting started in business, my father said something to me that, at first, sounded a little superficial. After being around for a while, however, I realized that he was right. He told me that part of being successful was just hanging in there and sticking with it. He said that many people quit too early, get impatient, fail to defer any gratification, and move around too much.

I had the advantage of loving what I was doing. So, in my early years, I didn't move around too much. I did defer plenty of gratification, I wasn't very impatient and I certainly didn't quit too early. And you know, my dad was absolutely right. After a while, people start to know who you are and what you do. You develop a reputation. And if people like you and you're competent, they begin to think of you as someone to do business with.

If you start a business but fail to stick around very long, you might not give your customers enough time to help you out. You won't have adequate time to develop your skills, learn the ropes, or develop a healthy reputation. If you get impatient and move around too much, or keep changing careers because you get bored or itchy for success, you may be quitting too early. You may not be giving your efforts enough time to show results. You may never quite get off the ground. But "getting off the ground" is often the most difficult part of the process, especially in entrepreneurial efforts. Often, when someone is very successful and it appears, on the surface, that they perform without effort, what you fail to see are the hundreds or even thousands of "presuccess" hours that created that sense of ease.

My wife, Kris, works in a networking business that serves as an excellent example. She knows that virtually anyone can be successful in her business, but that most people fail to give it a fair try. If they have one or two disappointments early on (which most do), they allow their fear or impatience to enter into the equation and they're on to something else. In a nutshell, they quit too early. They lack perseverance. Instead of saying, "This is going to take some time and work and I'm going to do what it takes," they believe that there is something out there that is going to be much easier. There isn't. Sometimes people will say to Kris, "You make it look so easy." What they don't realize is that it took a great deal of work to get to that point. Any new venture that is destined for success is going to take work and perseverance. If it didn't, your success wouldn't be as rewarding.

I've found that there is a delicate balance between being willing to stick something out and a willingness to make changes. You need the wisdom to know when to quit and when to stay right where you are. So, if you feel like quitting, don't do so impulsively. Instead, check in with your wisdom. If you're quitting too early, remind yourself to persevere.

83.

CONSIDER THE WISDOM OF OPTIMISM

There are essentially two types of people: optimists and pessimists. The question is, Which is wiser? Pessimists, of course, will tell you that they are being "realists." They insist that life is hard, things often don't work out, and it's not a good idea to set yourself up for disappointment. Pessimists believe that if you expect things to go wrong, you won't be let down when they do.

It should come as no surprise to you that pessimists experience far more disappointments than optimists. The reason is simple: They are looking for failure. They want verification that they are correct in their negative assumptions. They use negative experiences as ammunition and proof against the wisdom of optimism. They believe that optimists are burying their heads in the sand and that they simply don't understand the realities of life.

Optimists, however, understand that no one has a crystal ball and that no one can accurately predict the future. Along these lines, they know that although pessimists feel confident that things won't work out, they are only guessing and assuming that this is true. Optimists believe that, because no one *really* knows what's going to happen, it's far wiser and makes for a more pleasant and joyful experience of life if one is optimistic, if one assumes the best.

One of the most basic laws of success is that your energy follows your attention. This is true for every person on earth, optimists and pessimists alike, and whether you like it or not. If your energy is primarily negative; if you are looking for flaws, problems, and verification that life is essentially bad, that's where the bulk of your energy will lie. Your ability to manifest abundance will be severely limited because your energy will be directed, focused, and grounded in negativity and limitation. We create what we see and what we expect to see. If we enter into a situation with negative expectations, we will tend to create negative results.

Here's a simple, everyday example: I've been hired on numerous occasions to intervene in an argument. Invariably, the person who has hired me tells me all the negative qualities of the other person—he's stubborn, unwilling to listen, defensive, and obnoxious. He expects that our conversation will be heated and difficult. The person who has hired me enters the situation as an absolute pessimist, in every sense of the word. If you ask him, however, if he's being pessimistic, he would probably laugh at you. He feels he's simply being realistic.

I, on the other hand, enter the situation as an optimist. I've seen many situations like this and know without any doubt whatsoever that most people want to get along with others, and most people are capable of change. I enter into the situation looking for incremental improvement, areas of agreement, and common ground. I expect miracles.

The question is, Who has a better chance of success? Obviously, I do. The truth is that you not only *find* what you are looking for, you're *creating* it as well. When you're looking for answers and expect to find them, you usually do. Does this mean you'll always succeed? Absolutely not. But unlike the pessimist who will say, "See, what did I tell you? People are difficult and stubborn," the optimist will simply chalk it up as another learning experience. When I experience a failure in an interaction such as this one, I simply assume that it will be all that much easier next time because of all I have learned. There is a great deal of wisdom and joy in optimism. Give it a try.

84.

HOLD ON TIGHTLY, LET GO LIGHTLY

This is one of my very favorite sayings. "Hold on tightly, let go lightly" is a motto that encourages you to obtain the optimal balance between productivity and inner peace. "Hold on" suggests that you want to work hard, stick with things, give it your best shot, persevere, pursue your goals and never give up. The "let go lightly" side, however, suggests that you shouldn't hold on too long, and that when it is time to give in, give up, or let go, that you do so gracefully. Hold on tightly, let go lightly covers two very important aspects of success: the achievement of goals and the joy of happiness.

An excellent example of holding on tightly and letting go lightly exists in parenting. When we raise our children, most of us want to hold on tightly when they're young. We work very hard to protect them, to expose them to varied experiences. We defend their safety and their honor. We do all we can to steer them in the best possible direction. But then there comes a time when you need to "let go," when you need to set them free, to step aside and allow them to live their own lives. Letting go has nothing to do with ceasing to love our children. In fact, letting go is one of the ultimate expressions of a parent's love.

In business, and in all forms of competition, the same principle applies. It's appropriate and often necessary to do all we can to put the odds in our favor. Sometimes we need to negotiate hard, work in our best interest, expend effort like our life depends on it. We do everything we can to succeed. But then there comes a time when the season changes. Change is inevitable. Perhaps we have won—or lost—the game. Maybe we've played the game too long. Perhaps the industry has outgrown us, or we have outgrown our previous interests. This is when it's time to let go. If we do it gracefully, with perspective, we will remain peaceful and grow from our experience. Like opening a tight fist, we will feel free and energized. When the time does come to say good-bye, or to make a change, try doing so with grace. This will keep you pointed in the direction of your dreams. Instead of looking back, it will keep you focused on your next great adventure.

85.

BE WILLING TO APOLOGIZE

Whenever you are in business—or when you are taking risks, making things happen, interacting with others, or in the public eye—you are bound to make mistakes. At times you are going to use bad judgment, say something wrong, offend someone, criticize unnecessarily, be too demanding, or act selfishly. The question isn't whether you will make these mistakes—we all do. The question is, Can you admit to them? If so, the question becomes, Can you apologize?

Many people never apologize. They are either too self-conscious, self-righteous, stubborn, or arrogant to do so. The unwillingness to apologize is not just sad, it is a serious mistake as well. Almost everyone expects others to make mistakes. And with a humble and sincere apology, almost everyone is willing to forgive. However, if you are a person who is either unable or unwilling to apologize, you will be branded a difficult person to work with. And over time, people will avoid you, speak behind your back, and do nothing to help you.

The ability to apologize, to admit mistakes, is a beautiful human quality that brings people closer together and helps us succeed. By simply acknowledging our humanness and saying "I'm sorry" when appropriate, we bond with others and increase their trust in us.

On a live television talk show once I was discussing one of my books about happiness. I was in a terrible mood and was dealing with some pretty serious stuff myself. There was a guest on the show who was asking for my advice. Normally, this is where I'm at my best. I love talk shows and I love helping others when I can. I can't remember what I said on that particular day, but whatever it was, it offended him and hurt his feelings.

The producer contacted me with a rather nasty letter telling me that as far as she was concerned, I wasn't welcome on her show again! In years past, I think I would have become defensive, and offered an explanation in an attempt to make her a part of the problem. Instead, I simply offered my most sincere apology. I told her that I was wrong and that she was right. I really meant what I said. I even offered to call the guest I had offended if she could get me his number.

A few weeks went by and I received another letter from the producer. This time, however, the letter was quite different. She said that in over ten years as a producer, she had never received such a sincere and nondefensive apology. She asked if I would come back as a guest again real soon. By apologizing, I had corrected my mistake.

Obviously, you must never apologize as a tool of manipulation, to try to get a response like this or to get something out of it. I tell you this story to remind you of how forgiving people can be when you admit you're wrong. When you apologize from your heart, you keep most of your existing doors open. Occasionally, you may even open doors that had previously been closed.

86.

LIGHTEN UP

The only drawback to being a teacher of happiness is that, particularly in your own family, you have to do a good job at walking your talk! Otherwise you get ribbed and kidded, particularly by your children. When I get too uptight, for example, my youngest daughter, Kenna, reminds me frequently, "Daddy, don't sweat the small stuff."

It's really important for all of us to remember to lighten up, not to take life so incredibly seriously. When we do, we lose our perspective and sense of humor. We get caught up in all the problems, and hassles, and forget the joy of it all. In addition, when we get too serious, our attitude clouds our vision. Instead of being focused in the moment, and therefore at our personal best, our mind spins forward to future worries and backward to past regrets. It's important to take a few moments throughout the day to take a step back and see if you have your priorities in perspective. Are you taking your job or current project too seriously? Are you making a really big deal out of everything? Is it worth ruining your day over? Even when things are going wrong or when you're having a bad day, you don't have to turn it into "front-page news." You don't have to compound your misfortune by raising your blood pressure and beating your head against the wall.

I'm a firm believer that life doesn't have to be one giant emergency. I don't think you have to chase success, but you do need to slow down enough to let it catch up to you. Without question, abundance is there for the taking. There's enough to go around. When you're uptight, however, you forget this. You start to believe that the only way to succeed is to work extra hard, to roll up your sleeves and grind out another day. This isn't the case at all. One of the easiest and most enjoyable paths to success is to lighten up.

87.

REMEMBER THAT EVERYTHING IS USED
THE DAY AFTER YOU BUY IT

There's something special about buying a brand-new item. Whether it's a new car, a special piece of clothing, a new lawn mower, or any other consumer good, it's always nice to purchase it new. Unfortunately, however, there's often a huge price to pay. That price is what's called opportunity cost. Simply put, this is what you *could* have done with the money instead.

Everything is "used" the day after you buy it—and therefore less valuable. In the auto industry, they say a new car is no longer "new" the moment you drive off the lot. Have you ever bought something new and decided you didn't really want or need it and then try to sell it? If you're lucky, you'll get fifty cents on the dollar. I once bought a piece of exercise equipment for almost $1,000. I tried for weeks to sell it and was only able to get $300! I had only used it once. The truth is, you can usually buy a reasonable facsimile of an item—a car or anything else—and pay 30 to 50 percent less for it if you're willing to buy it used. And while it's not always critical to do so, and perhaps not as initially satisfying, there are a few ideas worth considering.

Consider a brand-new car. Let's assume you can purchase a new car for about $20,000. The moment you drive it off the lot, it loses a great deal of its so-called value, probably 10 to 15 percent, and continues to decline each month you own it. In addition, you'll probably be concerned about your hefty monthly payments, which will last for around five years, possibly even longer. That's sixty months of payments for something that is guaranteed to lose significant value each and every month. In addition to the payments you'll worry about damaging, scratching, and cleaning your new beauty, and there's always the possibility of theft. Then, there's insurance, registration, and maintenance to think about. In the end, there's a lot of money tied up in your new car. And perhaps a lot of unnecessary worry.

Your option, of course, is to purchase a used vehicle. Remember, everything is "used" the day after you buy it anyway. Nothing stays new very long. In addition to not worrying so much about theft and damage, your down payment, monthly payments, sales tax, insurance and registration costs will be far less with a used vehicle. If you are somewhat disciplined, and would like a worry-free investment, you could invest your savings (which would be simple to determine) in an appreciating asset. This way, with zero effort, you could save hundreds of dollars every month, guaranteed. Over your adult lifetime, this single decision made repeatedly, could help fund your retirement needs. I urge you to calculate the exact numbers or, if you don't know how, talk to someone who does. Your opportunity cost will surprise, perhaps even shock you!

I've met many people who have very little money at retirement. Yet some of these same people did manage to drive fairly nice cars, usually new ones, over the years. I wonder what would have happened if, instead of driving new cars and purchasing other new things, they would have invested their money more wisely.

88.

KEEP IN MIND THAT CHEAPER IS NOT
ALWAYS BETTER

The other side of the coin, however (from strategy #87), is that cheaper is not always better. Sometimes purchasing a used item (despite the potential advantages) is not worth the added time that's involved and the additional aggravation. The most obvious example might be the decision to purchase a "fixer-upper" house that is far cheaper than a newer one down the street. It might seem great that you're saving 30 percent (or more) on the initial cost. But unless you are qualified to fix things yourself and really love doing so, the cheaper home might drive you crazy. Older houses can, and often do, fall apart. And the repairs involved can be a real pain (and very expensive in the long run). Did you guess that I've made this mistake myself?

The same principle also applies to far more ordinary purchases. For example, it might be nice to save some money by purchasing a used computer instead of that brand-new one you like. However, if you can't use it very often because it's in the repair shop, you might *regret* the savings instead of appreciate them. Then there's the time involved in getting to and from the repair shop. Do you really want to spend your time attending to your used purchases?

It is not always simple to compute the actual cost of something. For example, at first blush, it seems like a $100 automobile tire that will last for 50,000 miles is exactly the same cost as a $50 tire that will last for just 25,000 miles. However, the devil is in the details. Consider, for example, the out-of-pocket cost of interest, of providing the additional $50 in tire investment for the length of time that you drive on the tire. Before you rush out and buy one $50 tire and replace it with another $50 tire, you have some other considerations. What is the value of your time in going in for one additional tire change? Then there are safety considerations. The point is, cheaper might be better, but then again, it might not be. Consider these decisions carefully.

Perhaps the best way to analyze the cheaper versus more expensive decision is to be completely honest about what you will do with the savings if you choose the cheaper version. Are you going to spend the savings? Are you really going to invest them? These decisions are more important than they appear on the surface. Over time, you can amass a fortune by making the best decision, most of the time.

89.

DON'T BE AFRAID TO TAKE BABY STEPS

Often, people worry about taking baby steps. They worry that the steps they are taking aren't big enough or significant enough. Or they worry that others will laugh at them, or see them as weak. Many people are so frightened to take baby steps that they end up doing nothing at all.

If success were easy, we'd all be successful. But while the strategies (like the ones in this book) that can take you toward success are simple, they aren't always easy. These strategies are only a road map; you must walk the path yourself.

I've had many people ask me the best way to write a book. My answer is almost always the same: just start writing. Don't wait. Even if you can only write a single paragraph, even a sentence, it's far better than nothing. There is a common misconception that if you wait to begin, someday you'll wake up with tremendous inspiration and take a giant step. I can assure you that this *is* possible, and it can happen to you. However, you greatly increase the likelihood of taking "giant steps" if you begin with baby steps. Both of my children started taking "baby steps" at around one year of age. Today, I can hardly keep up with them. Every process, be it personal or professional, begins with baby steps.

My wife and I decided a number of years ago to run a marathon together (yes, I'm proud of this). Our training began with twenty minutes of jogging per day—baby steps. It would have been crazy for us to wait to start our training program until we were able to run an hour. We never would have been able to do it; we needed our baby steps to succeed.

We've all heard people say, "I don't have enough money to start a savings plan. I can only afford to put $20 a week into my savings, or even $20 per month." My answer is: Great! Get started. Commit to putting 5 percent of your earnings into your savings. Take a baby step. Then, as you make more money, you'll be in the habit of saving. Your baby steps will have trained you how to do it. Chances are, if you avoid the baby-steps stage, you'll never take the bigger steps.

To become successful, it's critical to focus on what you can do, not on what you can't do. Baby steps are the vehicle, an essential part of the journey toward abundance. Maybe you'd like to start a business but feel you don't have the time to do everything that's required. No problem. Take some baby steps. Do something. Make that first phone call to City Hall about the license, or go to the library and pick up one book on some aspect of the business so that you can do some research. Or meet with one person a week—a mentor, perhaps—to get some ideas. Before you know it, those baby steps will become big steps.

90.

REMIND YOURSELF THAT YOUR LIFE ISN'T YOUR
ENEMY, BUT YOUR THINKING CAN BE

At times, it can seem like life is our enemy, as if things never quite pan out the way we would like them to, as if there's a secret conspiracy against us. However, it's critical to remember that, in reality, life *isn't* our enemy. There is no conspiracy. Life is just life. It is what it is. The factor that can make life *seem* like our enemy, however, is our thinking. Nothing more, nothing less. Life wants you to succeed just as much as it does the next person.

As obvious as this insight may seem, the implications are enormous. The truth is, life isn't going to accommodate any of us by giving us fewer demands, less traffic, people who are easier to get along with, or a smoother path toward success. If we want a different experience of life, a more peaceful outlook, we are the ones who must change.

If you're angry, you're the one having angry thoughts. If you're stressed, you're the one having stressful thoughts. If you're feeling sorry for yourself, again, you're the one having thoughts of self-pity. The good news, of course, is that while you can't alter life very often to suit your needs, you do have a fair measure of control over your own thinking. You can change the way you think, and you can change your reactions to life. It's entirely up to you. You can go on hating the many inconvenient aspects of life or you can relax and commit to changing your reactions to them.

It's very helpful to remind yourself (daily) that your life isn't your enemy. While you're at it, remind yourself of the tremendous power of

199

your own thinking, that your world is shaped by those thoughts you choose to focus on the most. You have the power to change your reactions, expectations, and outlook. You have the power to become anything you want to become. But to do so, you must realize that life is not your enemy; it's your friend.

91.

JUST DO IT

About ten years ago I was at a professional tennis tournament. It was a time when John McEnroe was at his peak and was seeded number one in the world. I was able, through friends, to be present at a series of players' interviews and it has always stuck with me.

The first interview was a player who lost in the first round of action. He was ranked pretty far down the ladder. When asked questions about his performance, he answered them articulately. He was quite precise about why he did certain things and why he made certain decisions.

The next interview was with John McEnroe. His answer to the question, How do you do it?, surprised me. He replied, "I don't really think about it. *I just do it.*" The really interesting part of the evening was that McEnroe's comments were not unique. In every instance, the *less* talented players accurately explained their form and strategy. The better the player, the less able they were to describe how they did what they do so well. In one way or another, the top players all said the same thing: We just do it. It didn't seem to come from arrogance or from a lack of intelligence, but from the perspective that too much thought about *how* you are going to do something interferes with actually going out and doing it. The top players in the world all shared the belief that the best way to do something is to just go out and do it.

As I reflect on top performers in other fields (and I understand that there are certainly exceptions), I do understand the wisdom in McEnroe's words. It's not that you don't want to be articulate, or that being able to describe your success or how you do something is bad, but there is something very powerful about just going out and getting started. One of the key benefits is that you can avoid much of the fear that others, who think everything through, experience.

Public speakers who plan out their speeches often experience stage fright. Those who simply trust in their abilities often do so with very little fear. This lack of fear is experienced by the audience as confidence. These speeches are usually well received. Salespersons who plan exactly what they're going to say can experience a great deal of fear because they're frightened they may forget their pitch. Also, the customer on the other end feels the "stiffness" of the planned presentation. It's stale and boring. On the other hand, salespeople who are spontaneous, who speak from the heart, who don't think too much about what they are going to say, can captivate their customers with their present-moment orientation. They are usually the top salespeople in their fields.

The next time you're about to begin something—new or familiar— avoid the temptation (within reason) of figuring out how you're going to do it. Especially important is to avoid telling others how you're going to go about it; you should trust that something within you, some form of intelligence, will kick in. You'll be surprised, if not amazed, at the results of this experiment. Sometimes it's hard to admit it, but just doing something is often quite a bit more effective than planning it out.

92.

RESIST THE TEMPTATION TO CONTINUALLY RAISE
YOUR STANDARD OF LIVING

Philosophically, there are two very different ways to become rich: (1) make more money, and (2) have fewer wants. In reality, there is a middle ground. I have found that the easiest way to assure an abundant life is to go ahead and make more money—and have a blast doing so—but avoid believing that, along with every pay increase, you must also raise your standard of living. To do so can be a foolish mistake.

Many people make more money than they ever dreamed possible, yet are more financially stressed than ever before. How can this be? Simple: What a vast majority of people do as they earn more money is to continue to spend as much if not more than they make. They buy a bigger home and a nicer car. They go on more expensive vacations, wear more expensive clothing, and eat at finer restaurants. They spend, spend, spend. Some go into foolish investments or silly tax shelters that don't hold up. Before you insist that you would never do this, I urge you to consider that you probably will—unless you consciously make a vow not to.

Making money is often easier than keeping it. The more you make, the more things you see that you want. The problem with material desire is that, unless you are extremely cautious, it is insatiable. Remember, more isn't necessarily better.

If you raise your standard of living to match your current income, it forces you to keep producing at the same level, whether you want to or not. And you may not want to. Never feeling as if you have "enough" causes several obvious problems. First, if you run into difficult times (which most people do at some point in their lives), pulling yourself out of a rut can be very difficult if you're spending everything you earn. If, however, you keep your spending and your desires in check, running into bad times will not cause an emergency. You'll simply make adjustments. The other major problem is that raising your standard of living, always wanting more, more, more, tends to keep you on the treadmill being busier and busier. The more things you have, the more things you have to take care of, insure, look after, protect, and worry about! Pretty soon, your life is filled with "stuff" and unnecessary demands on your time. You become "a servant to your servants."

This doesn't mean that you shouldn't have nice things or that you don't deserve them. But keep in mind that you also deserve a peaceful and happy life, and that material things don't necessarily make you happy! Happiness comes from within, by the way you relate to what you have, not from your actual possessions.

If you can manage to keep your desires in check, to live at or beneath your means, you'll discover a different type of abundance—peace. You'll be able to stay calm and relaxed. To me, this is among the greatest gifts in a lifetime.

93.

START A CAR POOL

Not everybody can make a car pool work, but a lot of people who can make it work simply do not make the effort, or are not fully aware of the hidden advantages. The first step is to get some information. Many communities have public agencies that match up potential car poolers. If an agency is not convenient, you can do it yourself.

Put a notice on the bulletin board where you work, including the time you arrive and leave and approximately where you live or where you'd like to be picked up. Or put a notice on the bulletin board where you live and include the area where you work.

The savings are overwhelming. Conservatively, it costs around thirty cents per mile to drive a car. This figure is the result of combining fixed expenses (those you incur whether you drive the car or not, such as interest on your car loan, age depreciation on the car, license fees, etc.) with variable expenses (those you incur when you actually drive, which include gas, oil, tires, mileage depreciation, bridge tolls, parking, and auto repairs).

For purposes of illustration, I will assume that your variable expense is about twenty cents per mile, although it might be somewhat higher depending on factors like the number of miles per gallon, whether you get free parking at work, the mileage depreciation, and so on.

Of course, some people drive a few blocks to work and others might drive fifty miles. For purposes of illustration, let's assume you drive only twenty miles per day, round-trip. If your mileage differs, just take the miles you actually drive and make an approximate adjustment.

Twenty miles round-trip cost about $4 per trip in variable expenses, or about $80 per month, or $960 per year. Because we're just estimating, let's round this to $1,000 per year (again, your number may well be quite a bit higher) driving from home to work as a solo driver. If you were to car pool with three other drivers, you would save $750 per year, and that savings is after taxes because the expense of driving from home to work is not deductible for income tax purposes.

In this simple example, if you invested that $750 in savings for thirty years and earned a reasonable rate of return on your investment, you would have saved a small fortune by the time you retire. If the numbers are larger, your savings will be larger, too.

There are additional significant benefits to be aware of in addition to the cost savings. Many large metropolitan areas have car pool lanes that can save drivers who share their cars up to *half* the time it takes to get to work. Think of the real value of your time. In some cases, you can save up to an hour a day off your round-trip commute time—that's 5 hours per week, or 250 hours per year! Can you imagine what you could do with that extra time? You could start your own home-based business, spend more time with your children, or keep it all to yourself. Finally, there are environmental factors to be aware of as well. When you share a ride to work, you consume far less gas and oil, which results in cleaner air. When you consider all the factors, I think you'll agree, this option is certainly worth looking into.

94.

HAVE A PLAN

It's quite difficult to get somewhere if you don't know where you're headed. Yet a huge percentage of us have no plan. We don't really know where we're going or how we're going to get there. It's easy to look and feel extremely busy when we don't have a plan, but in reality we're just spinning our wheels, putting out fires, or chasing our tails.

The other day I asked a gentleman who was working for a corporation in San Francisco, "Where would you like to be and what would you like to have accomplished a year from now?" His answer was somewhat typical. He said in a flustered tone, "I can't think that far ahead. I guess I'd just like to get through this mess." His "mess," of course, was his "in basket," his list of things to do. Unfortunately, getting through your daily task list doesn't necessarily lead you anywhere. In fact, it often leads you in circles. The very nature of an in-basket is that it's supposed to be full; items that are taken care of are constantly being replaced with new ones.

A plan is like a road map. It tells you where you are and points you in a direction. It helps you strategize about how you are going to get from point A to point B. For example, if your goal is to increase your productivity or sales volume by 50 percent, your plan would be a daily reminder of the steps necessary to achieve that goal. Part of your plan, for instance, might be to make phone calls to five new potential customers daily, rather than simply returning the phone calls that come your way. Or part of your plan might be to take three new courses to increase your knowledge base before the end of the year. Without this predetermined plan, it is probable that you wouldn't find the time to take any courses. Like the gentleman I spoke to from San Francisco, you'd be too busy putting out daily fires. You'd keep thinking, "I'll get to it later." But somehow you never will.

When you have a predetermined plan, something magical happens: Your plan helps you to draw out your inner strength, creativity, and discipline. In some mysterious way, you are usually able to stick to your plan, once you have one in place. A few years ago, I suggested to a single mom who was struggling with her finances that she needed a financial plan. She hadn't been able to save a dime for her eventual retirement. She said she had been waiting for the right time to start saving, but there never seemed to be anything left over at the end of the month. The plan she came up with took her about five minutes to create, but was among the most significant five minutes of her life. She decided that if she didn't start saving now, she may never begin. So she committed to pay herself first. She said that her "plan" was to save 10 percent of every dollar she earned and put it toward her retirement. I bumped into her a while ago and asked her how it was going. She reported that she was well on her way toward financial freedom. Her plan had, in her words, saved her life. She insisted that, once she had a plan in place, following it was easy.

With a plan in mind, the sky's the limit. As long as you can visualize a way to implement your plan, your dreams—however big—can become a reality. Your plan may be to become a multimillionaire, to run a marathon, to spend an extra day each week with your children, or to open an ice-cream shop. It doesn't matter what your plan is, but it does matter that you have one. Make a plan today.

95.

DON'T GET LOST IN YOUR PLAN

On the other end of the spectrum from *not* having a plan is someone who gets *lost* in their plan. This, too, is easy to do. It's easy to become focused, even obsessed with your plan or your goals. You can become so engrossed in your plan that you forget to enjoy the process. One of my favorite quotes says, "Life is what's happening while we're busy making other plans." What a powerful message!

Many people get lost in their dreams of becoming successful. So much so that they sacrifice their relationships with family members, friends, even themselves. They are focused on the end result, not on the steps along the way. The steps, however, are where you find the joy.

There are several reasons why people become obsessed with their plans and future goals. Perhaps most important is that people worry too much about their success and the direction of their lives. Keep in mind that worrying interferes with your ability to create abundance; it gets in the way and clouds your vision. Becoming successful is not difficult. In fact, creating success is virtually inevitable when you get *out* of your own way. And as we have been discussing throughout this book, worry and lack of faith are your greatest obstacles. When you take worry out of the picture, your plan will have a chance to unfold.

Keep in touch with your sense of knowing, that inner awareness that any goal or dream you have, as long as you know what it is, is within your grasp. An important aspect of a successful life is achieving a balance between these two seemingly different messages (having a plan, but not getting lost in it). My advice is for you to know exactly where you'd like to go and exactly how you plan to get there. But at the same time, let go of your goal and enjoy the ride. Each step of your journey is an important part of your unique curriculum. Each hurdle you face and problem you overcome is part of your divine plan. So don't get lost in your plan. If you do, you'll not only interfere with the very goals you'd like to achieve but you'll also miss out on all the fun.

96.

STOP COMMISERATING

Commiserating is a socially accepted form of complaining. Yet in reality it's exactly the same thing. We all do it, only to different degrees. People commiserate for several reasons. First, it's a habit. Everyone else is doing it, too. Next, many people feel they are getting somewhere or getting some benefit when they do it. Finally, some people think "getting things off their chest" or allowing others to do so is a positive action. They associate the familiarity of commiseration with a feeling of relief.

Unfortunately, commiseration is a bad habit and it detracts from your success and from the success of others. Our actions follow our energy, which includes our thinking and our conversations. Negative conversations, complaining and commiserating are expressions of negativity.

The next time you're at a social gathering listen carefully to all the commiseration in the room. Listen to the ways people share their misery and wallow in their problems. Feel the energy of it all. Then, when you get home, sit quietly for a few minutes and consider what just happened. Try to tally up, in your mind, all the commiserating and all the complaints. Now ask yourself: How much good does it all do? How far does it go toward solving problems, creating opportunity, expressing joy, and bringing forth creativity? The answer is none, zero, zip. It does no good. But it's actually far worse than that. The amount of energy the average person spends in commiseration is awesome! Listen to the conversations around you—at work, over lunch, at home. It's everywhere and it's a rare person who chooses not to participate. However, the one person in twenty who makes this decision has a tremendous advantage over everyone else.

Consider the amount of mental and emotional energy expended in commiseration. It's a lot. This is energy that could be spent in creative ideas or quiet reflection. This is energy that might be used to solve a problem, implement an idea, or market a product. This energy is the source of your abundance. It's yours, and it's free. When you make the decision to stop commiserating, you free up this energy—instantly. New thoughts begin to emerge; new, exciting ideas rise to the surface.

Make no mistake about it: Breaking this habit is difficult. It takes time, but it's worth it. The only way to quit is to notice yourself in the midst of commiseration or when you're about to commiserate. Gently remind yourself that, while it's tempting to join the others, you've got better things to do and dreams to pursue. As you avoid the tendency to commiserate, your rewards will be swift and certain.

97.

WORK AT IT

You probably haven't found anything in this book too difficult to understand. Perhaps, for the most part, you have had the feeling of "Oh, I already know that." So one of my concluding thoughts as we near the end of this book is something you may not already know.

Perhaps the most difficult insight about how to save money, create abundance, have a wonderful life, and accumulate wealth is that, although it's fun and simple, you do have to work on it. These dreams, although within the grasp of anyone, do not necessarily come naturally.

We can break tasks into two basic categories: There are those tasks we know we have to study and learn, and then there are those we believe just come naturally. To build a suspension bridge obviously requires a lot of specific learning, and to breathe comes naturally from birth. Now, here's the question: Does abundance come naturally like eating and breathing, or is it a task that must be learned and worked? I think it's a little of both.

Let's take an analogous issue. Does parenting come naturally or is it something that must be learned and worked? Often a parent produces a rebellious, angry child—a child that cannot maintain relationships, survive in school, keep a job, and so on. There are very few parents, however, who would admit they did a bad job of parenting, and I'm almost sure that there is no parent who sits up late at night planning how to be a bad parent. I believe that every parent would be sincere in a statement that he or she was a good parent, even if their child is sitting out a sentence in a juvenile detention facility. Certainly, the economic and industrial situation is a contributor in the difficulties we face as parents, but another big contributor is that many parents just don't know how to parent! So, if parents can be misled about their ability to parent, is it possible that parents can be equally misled about their ability to save money, make dreams come true, and accumulate wealth?

I believe that the pursuit of an abundant life includes a little of both. It's a natural process, but it does take some work. The best and most empowering ideas are simple, but they require implementation. I believe I am empowering you when I tell you that it's *your* choice. If you fail to save money and accumulate wealth, you can blame others and the world. Or you can gain some insight about your own contribution. Once you have insight about your part in the process, you can open the door and have the opportunity to do something about it. This is a powerful and important door to open. You have the power to create the life of your dreams. Go ahead and make it happen!

98.

CREATE YOUR OWN LUCK

Some people seem to get all the luck. Upon closer examination, however, you'd be shocked at the amount of "luck" that is self-created. The truth is, while luck is a factor of success from time to time, "lucky people" share some very consistent characteristics.

Lucky people are constantly putting themselves in the position to be lucky. In other words, they step up to the plate, they participate, they tell others that they are willing to accept help. I was "lucky" in a finance course I took at Pepperdine University many years ago. My friends couldn't believe that the professor gave me an A for the course when it seemed like I probably deserved a B at best. What they didn't know was that I visited the professor and solicited his help *every single day* that he had office hours. The professor knew, with no doubt whatsoever, that I was trying hard and that I knew the material. Was I lucky? Sure I was, but had I not demonstrated a burning desire to learn, I wouldn't have been nearly so lucky. The professor wouldn't have even known me, much less cared if I succeeded. As it was, however, my professor really liked me. He wanted me to succeed. In fact, it was almost as important to him as it was to me. He knew I was sincere, not only in my efforts to learn but also in my fondness for him as a person and in my respect for him as an instructor. Obviously, I was in a position to be lucky.

Since that time, I've been lucky hundreds of times. I've been really lucky, for example, to get on certain radio and television shows around the country to promote my work. But while others complain about their lack of promotion and/or wait for the phone to ring, I'm busy sending books, press kits, and show ideas to producers all over the country, sometimes several times a day for months and months at a time. Am I lucky? You bet I am! But I create a great deal of that luck myself by letting people know I'm ready and willing to be lucky.

I have an acquaintance who just got his "big break" in the corporate world. "He's so lucky," everyone said. And they're absolutely right: He was lucky. But was it blind luck or did the fact that he arrived at the office before most people had gotten out of bed, or that he remembered his boss's birthday (and his children's), or that he was willing to apologize when he was wrong, shared the credit when he deserved all of it, said "thank you" when something nice came his way, and persevered long after others gave up have something to do with it? I think both are true. He *was* lucky, but he also put himself in the position to be lucky. Creating your own luck is sort of like planting a garden in an ideal environment. You'll be "luckier" with your plants if you provide the best soil, water, sunshine, and growing conditions. If you don't do these things, you might still get lucky and have a bumper crop, but the odds are far less likely.

The strategies in this book are designed to put you in a position to become lucky. As you look back and reread the various sections, you'll notice that most of the strategies are designed to give you an edge, improve your attitude, help make you a kinder or less reactive person, sharpen your wisdom, or deepen your perspective. The truth is, you never really know where your lucky breaks are going to come from. Lucky people know this, so they always act as if luck is just around the corner. Perhaps the person you choose to smile at or help, instead of frown at and ignore, is in a position to help you—or will be some day. You never know. As you take the advice in this book to heart, you'll notice that luck will begin to come your way. Then others will be calling you lucky.

99.

DON'T FORGET TO HAVE FUN

Obviously, this hasn't been a book on how to improve the rate of return in your investment portfolio. It's not an investment strategy book, or a book on finance or economics. It's a book on how to create abundance, how to manifest your dreams. I believe that the advice in this book can help you much more than any book on finance or economics. I wrote this book not only to help you make your dreams come true, but also to help you maximize enjoyment, the quality of your life, and the potential for fun. I want you to succeed, and I know you can. But just as important, I want you to have fun. And the more fun you have—when mixed with wisdom, creativity, and a little hard work—the more you are going to succeed.

When you look back on your life, perhaps on your deathbed or toward the end, it's very likely that you *won't* be asking yourself how much money you made or how many possessions you managed to collect. Nor will you see the purpose of life as being the collection of achievements or even the fulfillment of your goals. What you will see, I believe, is that the purpose of life was to have been kind and loving, to grow and to give back to others. You will have plenty of regrets if you forget to have fun, and probably none if you do not.

Realizing your dreams—whatever they are—can be a blast. It's certainly enjoyable to feel financially secure, but even more so to use your mind, attitude, charm, wisdom, and genuine kindness to create great abundance in all aspects of your life.

As you reflect on the strategies in this book, accept them into your life in the spirit in which they are offered—lighthearted, helpful, and fun. The more fun you have, the more you are likely to succeed. Don't listen to the so-called experts who tell you that creating wealth is a serious venture. Sure, it's hard work, but that's a different matter entirely. This is your life. You have the right to enjoy it. So be successful and create great abundance, but don't forget to have fun!

100.

DON'T SWEAT THE SMALL STUFF!

Probably the hardest part of writing this book was the decision about how to bring it to an end. Whether you have read my earlier book *Don't Sweat the Small Stuff* or not, I couldn't resist bringing the subject to your attention. This is because, to me, the decision to not sweat the small stuff lies at the heart of a high-quality life. It helps you to keep your perspective and to maintain a lighthearted nature and a positive outlook on life.

Life is so full. There are so many things to deal with on a day-to-day, moment-to-moment basis, and so many demands on our time. Often, however, because we allow ourselves to get all worked up about things that really aren't that big a deal, we lose not only our effectiveness but our enjoyment of life as well. If you can learn to be one of the few people who refuses to sweat the small stuff, you will have created an enormous edge for yourself in your life. Rather than expending energy being bothered, annoyed, and frustrated, you'll use that energy for creativity, problem solving, and the creation of abundance.

Sometimes we forget that the way we relate to our problems has a lot to do with how quickly and effectively we solve them. We forget that when we see life as a great big emergency, when we are uptight, frustrated, and stressed, that our vision is clouded and our wisdom suffers. We end up making more mistakes, wasting energy, and making poor decisions.

When you don't sweat the small stuff, your life won't be perfect, but your chances for success will be greatly enhanced and the quality of your life will soar. Instead of being distracted by the daily annoyances and irritations that each of us must face, you'll be able to keep your bearings and your perspective. You'll realize that, from a larger point of view, you're a very lucky person and that to sweat the small stuff is to forget to be grateful for this precious gift of life. I hope this book has been and will be helpful to you in the creation of your dreams. I wish you the very best of everything.

Treasure yourself.

If you'd like to share with me the simple ways in which you create abundance and joy in your own life, please write me—and include a self-addressed stamped envelope—at P.O. Box 1196, Orinda, CA 94563. Thank you.

SUGGESTED READING

Allen, James. *As a Man Thinketh*. New York: Barnes & Noble, 1992.

Carlson, Richard. *You Can Be Happy No Matter What*. San Rafael, Calif.: New World Library, 1992.
———. *You Can Feel Good Again*. New York: Plume 1993.
———. *Short Cut Through Therapy*. New York, Plume: 1995.
———. *Don't Sweat the Small Stuff*. New York: Hyperion, 1997.

Carnegie, Dale. *How to Stop Worrying and Start Living*. New York: Pocket Books, 1984.

Cates, David, *Unconditional Money*, Willamina, Ore.: Buffalo Press, 1995.

Chopra, Deepak. *The Seven Spiritual Laws of Success*. San Rafael, Calif.: New World Library, 1994.
———. *Creating Affluence*. New York: New World Library, 1993.

Covey, Stephen R. *The Seven Habits of Highly Effective People*. New York: Fireside, 1989.

Day, Laura. *Practical Intuition*. New York: Villard, 1996.

Dyer, Wayne. *Real Magic*. New York: HarperCollins, 1992.

Givens, Charles. *Wealth Without Risk*. New York: Simon & Schuster, 1991.

Gross, Daniel. *Forbes Greatest Business Stories of All Time*. New York: John Wiley & Sons, 1996.

Hansen, Mark Victor. *Out of the Blue*. New York: HarperCollins, 1996.

Hill, Napoleon. *Think and Grow Rich*. New York: Fawcett Columbine, 1937.

Jeffers, Susan. *Feel the Fear and Do It Anyway*! New York: Fawcett Columbine, 1987.

Kushner, Harold. *When All You've Ever Wanted Isn't Enough*. New York: Pocket Books, 1986.

Machtig, Brett. *Wealth in a Decade*. Chicago: Irwin Professional Publishing, 1997.

Mandino, Og. *The Greatest Salesman in the World*. New York: Bantam, 1972.
———. *Secrets of Success and Happiness*. New York: Fawcett Columbine, 1995.

McCormack, Mark H. *What They Don't Teach You at Harvard Business School*. New York: Bantam, 1984.

Novak, Michael. *Business as a Calling*. New York: The Free Press, 1996.

Phillips, Michael. *The Seven Laws of Money*. Boston: Shambhala, 1997.

Ribeiro, Lair. *Success Is No Accident*. New York: St. Martin's Press, 1996.

Shinn, Florence Shovel. *The Secret Door to Success*. Marina Del Ray, Calif.: DeVorss & Company, 1940.
———. *The Game of Life and How to Play It*. New York: Fireside, 1986.

Sinetar, Marsha. *To Build the Life You Want, Create the Work You Love*. New York: St. Martin's Griffin, 1995.

Sternberg, Robert. *Successful Intelligence*. New York: Simon & Schuster, 1996.

Toppel, Edward Allen. *Zen in the Markets*. New York: Warner, 1992.